Obstacles Equal Opportunities

Compiled by Heather Andrews

Compiled by Heather Andrews:

http://publishing.followitthru.com/

www.followitthru.com

Book and cover design by Jennifer Insignares: www.yourdesignbyjen.com

Editing by Amanda Horan: www.amandahoranediting.com

Formatting by Bojan Kratofil: https://www.facebook.com/bojan.kratofil

Manuscript compilation by Julie Kapuschak: www.juliemaye.com

Audiobook production by Carrie-Ann Baron: www.tenaciousliving.org

Audiobook production by Vladimir Krstic: www.supersonicproductions.net

Audiobook narration by Noelle Leemburg: www.bsavvy.ca

ISBN: 978-1- 5136-2128- 9

Gratitude

In October 2016, I was invited to be part of a co-authored book. I felt vulnerable and extremely nervous. I knew if I wrote a chapter about myself for that book, I would be stepping way beyond my comfort zone.

I wondered what people—especially my own kids—would think of me sharing my personal story and publishing it for the world to read.

I pushed my fears aside and plunged myself into the opportunity instead. I wrote a book chapter! I opened myself up to a whole new world. Allowing myself to face a challenge that made me feel vulnerable gave me the incredible healing experience of putting one of my most formative life experiences into words on a page. I discovered the power of connection by sharing that collaboration with seventeen co-authors.

Only later did I learn how the book's publishers, Kate Gardner and Kim Boudreau Smith, would mentor me.

When that book hit the international bestseller list on Amazon in December 2016, I could not believe it. That moment changed my business and my life.

Soon after, Kate Gardner launched her publishing mentorship mastermind and accepted me. I was over the moon.

My gut instinct was screaming at me to publish a book to help people share experiences of how they overcame incredible obstacles, how they found courage, and what they learned on their journey. The premise was for these authors to share their stories, courage, and hope, and let people who are in a dark place know they aren't alone. You are reading the result of that gut instinct.

I am so grateful for the opportunity that Kate provided to publish this collaborative book, to learn how to be a publisher and to share this wonderful experience with rising authors.

I am grateful for the co-authors who chose publishing in this book. They opened their hearts, showing trust and vulnerability when they shared their stories with the world. They are amazing humans who love where their lives are at because they embraced the obstacles and saw them as opportunities to grow, to overcome and to live the lives they wanted.

I'm grateful to Carrie-Ann Baron and Vladimir Krstic for their project management and production of the audiobook. Their dedication and patience ensured that our voices would be heard. I am also thankful for Noelle Leemburg, who partnered with Carrie-Ann (fellow co-author) and myself to bring our words to life.

I am grateful for my family: my husband, my mom, the loving memory of my dad and my three wonderful teenagers who have loved and supported me since the beginning of my journey in 2015 when I launched my business after a devastating job loss.

I am thankful for my friends who supported me, believed in me and offered their unconditional love when the days were dark.

I am especially thankful for the coaches who saved a space for me to rise, Carolin Soldo, Ramona Remesat, Belinda Ginter and Noelle Leemburg. I appreciate you so much. You all taught me different skillsets and believed in me when I doubted myself. Thank you for showing me how to love my life again and discover who I am!

I wish you all the bravery, healing and courage in the world to go out and be unapologetically YOU!

Hugs always,

Heather

Table of Contents

Foreword

It was September of 2015 when I met Heather Andrews for the first time.

We joined forces to make Heather's dream of running a thriving, full-time coaching business a reality. Our journey began with clarity and lots of soul searching to discover Heather's passion and purpose.

Today, I am honored and proud to be her coach. Heather has transformed herself from a fledgling entrepreneur who lacked focus and felt overwhelmed to knowing exactly what she wants, confidently speaking her truth, and making bold decisions to make her dreams come true. This is what success is all about. It takes a woman with self-worth, confidence, and guts to stand up for her vision.

Heather had worked in the healthcare sector for twenty-five years, giving her an insider's view of what ignoring one's health looks like, before she became a health coach. Her own life experience showed her how important it was to be able to help others avoid a life dominated by chaos and stress. With all this in mind, together we created a new brand—Follow It Thru—to encompass Heather's coaching programs and promote it with a thoughtful and authentic marketing strategy.

She knows that mastering positive habits is proven to be an effective approach to making lifestyle changes last. She's married to an American war veteran and has three kids, so you can imagine the difference healthy habits make in her household.

Heather's photo should be in the dictionary under 'working mom.' While creating and running her business, she's built stronger relationships with her children and husband while decreasing the household chaos. She's raising healthy teenagers despite the plethora of temptations in their world.

Heather's path to success included mastering the fundamentals of business, but there is more to success than a great vision. Heather recognized the need to do essential inner work to ensure the success of her dreams.

Self-discovery, building confidence and finding her voice were the hardest parts—and the most important—to taking her business to the next level. Those inner changes led her to revamp her entire life and discover her ultimate mission: helping other moms live stellar lives.

Today, Heather knows who she is. In 2016, she stepped onstage at my annual conference and shared her message with a room full of entrepreneurial women for the first time. That day, she not only connected with other women who saw the value in taking back control of their lives and their health, but she also further reinforced her dedication to living authentically.

Since then, Heather has continued to speak to corporate, health and women's groups and hosts talks for women looking to re-balance their lives. Her message resonates deeply with her fellow 'moms on the go,' who felt helpless and lost before meeting her. Women from around the world flock to her to find encouragement and power in her message.

If you are looking for your real purpose and the power to transform your life and yourself, then this book is for you. Heather is an expert in her field and teaches from years of real-life experience. She knows what it means to power through and follow her mission.

Heather took her life from self-doubt and chaos, to a life full of purpose and belief, in which she unapologetically makes her mission and vision a reality. Heather and I both believe that a woman should never stay stuck in a life that doesn't fully light her up.

I am so proud of what Heather has accomplished in the past year alone. What started as her business-coaching journey has turned into a path of deeper self-discovery and transformation from the inside out.

I run an international coaching business, and my mission is to help women go from Passion to Profits®. The best part of my job is empowering women to be their best selves and watching them turn into powerhouses with the ability to impact the world. Because of Heather, I get to live on purpose every day and follow my own mission. I will be forever grateful and proud to be her mentor.

While designing her life with intention, Heather is on her way to the top. Her clients benefit from her wisdom and authenticity. I am excited to see the continued impact Heather will make in this world with her books, speaking and coaching.

You're blessed to have found this book and Heather's message. Let it inspire you to do more, be more and discover the best version of yourself.

With love and gratitude,

Carolin Soldo

www.carolinsoldo.com

Introduction

This book could not exist without my three children.

No, they didn't type it up or check my spelling. They did something indispensable to making this book dream into a reality.

Shane, Tessa, and Spencer taught me to embrace life to its fullest. They are my reason for doing everything I do, for achieving my dreams, and for being a better human.

I'm biased, but they're amazing.

I never thought I would be a mom. I was career-driven from a young age, and kids just weren't on my mind. When I met their future father—an American soldier—in the middle of the Saudi Arabian desert, I knew my life would be far from ordinary. When I became pregnant for the first time, I was happy and excited, but I had no idea how I was going to be a good mom. Maybe you never know for sure as a parent if everything you're doing is right, but twenty years and three teenagers later, it seems like everything has turned out well. My kids are my inspiration every day. I think they teach me more than I teach them.

Mom, I will make my own success!

—Shane Andrews

Mom, the things you teach me daily, I will remember forever.

—Tessa Andrews

Mom, I failed, and I know what that feels like. I will work hard and improve. I love you!

—Spencer Andrews

Their statements throughout the years will stay with me forever because they have inspired me to go after my dreams: to start my own coaching and publishing business. I've always believed I can model the way for my kids and they will learn by example. In starting my own business, I knew I could fail, but I saw it as a chance to learn for myself and to teach my kids. I knew I could create the potential I feel in my heart.

When the opportunity presented itself to compile and publish this book, all I could think was, "Hell, yeah!" Yes, it would be a huge undertaking. But it aligned so perfectly with my vision that I couldn't ignore the feeling in my gut that said, "Do it!"

I wanted to create an opportunity for others to know they are not alone in their world. I have felt very much alone many times in my life during the darkest of times. I don't wish that on anyone.

My vision for this book is to provide courage when the days seem dark. The days when getting out of bed is the best you can hope for.

I wanted to share with others the lessons learned from those who have overcome adversity before them. Life can change for the better, and you can be an agent of that change.

The co-authors of this book, women, and men, have known loss, tragedy, trauma, disease, and failure. Bottomed out, they found courage, support, and belief in themselves. Step by small step, they moved forward, hoped for better days as they lived through the struggles they faced and the unique obstacles life had put in their path. They believed things could be different, found in their hearts the courage to ask for help or looked deep inside to find the strength to move from darkness to light.

Their stories are real and heartfelt. These authors have shared an inside glimpse of their lives with you and the lessons they learned that changed their lives. Though each of their paths was different, all of them learned that life is about the journey. We are meant to experience life as a team sport. You are not alone on your path.

Feel the power of each story. You are welcome to reach out to the authors you feel a connection with. Our wish for you as our reader is to learn, be courageous and grow so that you can see a path to your own stellar life.

Heather Andrews

Heather is a lifestyle strategist who helps women to live the stellar life they deserve. She's driven to help women learn to say YES to a better life, by saying NO to the obstacles in their path.

Heather has a career, an online business, and is raising three teenagers! When her husband was deployed to Afghanistan, she created the secret formula to raising children as a solo parent.

With her experience and certifications as a healthcare professional, manager, change mentor, and health coach, she is the founder of Follow It Thru Health Coaching and creator of the MOM on the Go program.

Eager to help others share their stories of inspirational change, Heather is publishing a forthcoming compilation book, coming December 2017.

Find Heather online:

www.followitthru.com
http://publishing.followitthru.com
www.facebook.com/groups/empoweredmoms123

Chapter 1

What Happened to My Identity?

By Heather Andrews

I was leading a staff meeting when I got the call from HR. My gut had been telling me for a while that the call was coming. As I designated my replacement in the meeting, I mentally steeled myself and proceeded to human resources.

After twelve years of service, including spending the last three years in my dream job, suddenly I was being told my role had been 'restructured' out of existence. The management role I had been groomed for over the years was deleted like a typo in an inter-office memo. The job I had prioritized over my family and my health- eliminated. A position that had, for months now, led me to tearfully phoning my mom on my commute home and yelling at my kids for no reason, suddenly didn't exist.

I was numb. Looking back, I just had no idea how to process what had happened. It wasn't the layoff on its own that bothered me. Layoffs happen all the time. It was something else. I had knotted my identity into the three words that made up my job title and the six figures in my salary. Who was Heather Andrews if she wasn't an irreplaceable cog in a corporation watered with her sweat and tears? What was she worth?

Why had I given them so much power over my life, my future, and my financial stability when I could be replaced in a heartbeat?

The HR staffer (the kind they hire so that nobody who likes you has to look you in the eye when they cut you loose) offered to call me a taxi to get home. I declined. I could get myself home, thank you very much. HR escorted me out of the building with a box of my belongings. I'd left something behind, but I wouldn't realize what that 'something' was for another twelve painful months.

I cried alone in my car, not for myself, but for the friends that remained who were yet to be restructured. Especially the ones who had been there for thirty-plus years with limited options for future employment. They were my friends first, co-workers second. I was their leader; we'd shared our successes and failures and relied on each other for support. All gone.

Feeling utterly forsaken, I took a deep breath and shifted into survival mode as I left the staff parking lot for the last time.

I was a pro at survival mode. It's what helped me get through my husband's deployment to Afghanistan, when I was left to raise our three children without going crazy. Back then, I developed systems and strategies to keep the four of us happy and healthy. Survival mode meant worrying about everyone else before I could worry about myself. As I drove myself home, I was hurt, full of disbelief, confused and angry; but instead of feeling it, I tucked it away. *I will not be judged as a failure*, I thought. *I will show them.*

This time around, survival mode meant finding my financial footing immediately. I'm a resourceful gen-Xer. I'd built my resume through diverse positions in healthcare so that I could be agile in a world that valued a variety of skill sets.

I began a health coaching certificate program within a week of being restructured out of existence. It was supposed to be part of my five-year exit strategy from my job. I knew health coaching would be a positive step forward. I had proven I knew how to help people avoid the tailspin I'd fallen into before I figured things out following John's deployment. I threw myself into becoming a health coach and ignored my own wound that was still super raw.

A couple of weeks after my layoff, I also hustled to get some contract work in my field so I could feed my family, all the while burying a deeply unsettling feeling that something was missing. The financial footing was so important to me. I may not have been able to control much at that point, but I could at least bring home a paycheck.

In my industry, news travels fast. Everyone in my new workplace knew I'd been laid off. I couldn't help feeling that behind their friendly faces, they were judging me, guessing what I did wrong that got me restructured. I felt like an outsider. A loser.

However, I kept my head above water. My health coaching certification went really well, and I hired a top-notch business coach to help me develop my coaching business. My coach was amazing. She helped me see my story and life experience in a new light and created space for me to build a business around being a busy mom and helping others use the same techniques I used when John was in Afghanistan.

For a while, things seemed to go well—until they didn't.

About a year into building my business, I stalled. I worked constantly, still doing contract work in addition to being an entrepreneur. I'd checked all the boxes required for my business to thrive, yet I struggled to get clients.

I started making excuses for what seemed to be an impending failure. *Why should I put myself out there if I'm just going to get on trampled again?* I busied myself with just about anything other than moving my business forward. I set boundaries that kept me in and everyone else out.

It was hard to be motivated to go out in public when I had lost so many friends. It seemed like all those work friends who supported me immediately after I had lost my job were afraid layoffs were contagious. I'd never felt so lonely.

It was a confusing time. Partly, I was motivated to create my business, and I loved every minute of coaching. At the same time, I didn't have a reason for doing it much beyond making an income. I had no idea what I stood for.

My 'why' was the most important piece of why I did what I did. However, I was too caught up in how I was going to do it to even vaguely consider my 'why.'

Then, my coach presented me with an opportunity. She was hosting a big event in Miami focused on transformation and invited me to speak. I accepted.

I put a ton of not-so-helpful pressure on myself to make the most of my speaking opportunity and my time at the conference. It would be my first chance to speak to my business in a public forum, the first time my husband could see me in full entrepreneur mode out in the wild and a chance to prove to myself that I was carving the right path.

My Miami talk went… ok.

My performance wasn't perfect, but through my talk, I connected with some people and began to build relationships that would pay off big later. Something was off the whole time, though. When

I was on stage or talking to people afterward, I didn't feel like me. I felt inauthentic, like I was selling someone else's business in someone else's skin.

I was trying to present a perfect person to the world, but I did not feel like that perfect version of Heather. Not a bit. I felt angry.

That disconnect made one thing very clear: perfect Heather didn't exist and I had to stop pretending she did. I had to find the real Heather instead, and I definitely needed to tweak my business so I could speak to it with full authenticity, whatever that meant for me.

I started to remember there was 'something' I'd left behind the day I was laid off a year earlier.

Back home, I began working with a mindset expert. Total game changer. She saw what I hadn't: what I lost the day I lost my job.

I'd lost my identity. That revelation changed everything.

People in my life had been telling me to get over the job loss. "People lose jobs every day. It's time to move on, Heather."

However, my mindset coach saw it differently. "They took something from you the day they escorted you out the door, Heather," she said. She wasn't talking about my title or my income. "They took your power and your self-worth, and you need to get that back."

Oh my gosh. Suddenly, it all made sense.

How had I not realized how much of my worth I'd put into that damn job title? Of course I felt like a loser! I'd invested almost all of what made me, me into this external mechanism like I was feeding quarters into a happiness vending machine. My return on this investment was paltry. No wonder I felt that committing myself to anything ever again (even a business I really cared about) was a waste of time and energy.

The powerful version of Heather who thrived behind the job title—a confident, proud, empowered leader of teams who got shit done—still existed. I just had to find her again.

Easier said than done.

The current version of Heather had an abundance of self-doubt and negligible self-worth. Where the job title had defined me before, I let the lack of the job title continue to define me. I cried for four days when I realized how long I held onto that pain and how deeply hurt I was.

For more than a year, I'd tried to brush off the job loss, but to get through it, I had to accept that I hadn't just lost a job. I mourned the person I was in that job, the career path I'd been on and the network I built around me. Restarting my career after being so proud of how high I climbed was rough; doing it in plain sight made it even harsher.

To heal, I had to acknowledge that I was at the bottom of a deep well. Next, I needed to decide not to stay stuck there alone in the dark, damp cold.

It took a significant investment in healing myself on the inside before I rebuilt the self-worth that had shattered fourteen months earlier. I had to either react to the situation or let it defeat me.

External motivation is unsustainable. No wonder I was so angry and helpless. When one thing in your life is screwed up, chances are everything else is out of alignment too. I needed to build my self-esteem from the ground up in a way that respected my work, achievements, and abilities on their own merits.

I had to be willing to do the work to make change happen. I had to drag myself forward, inch-by-inch before I could crawl, crawl before I could walk and walk before I could run the marathon ahead. More importantly, I needed to be willing to learn. If you stop learning, you may as well be dead.

So I learned. In time, I learned that I was worthy to be a coach, a business owner, to have credibility and to strive for something better. That learning was key to my growth. Without my self-worth, I didn't know who I was, and I couldn't show up in my own business without a strong sense of identity and belief in myself.

The self-worth healing process was underway when I was invited to write a chapter in a book about successful businesses. I had to rewind about ten years and distil everything that had gotten me to where I was. Putting it all down on paper was huge. I'd shown myself how much of an impact I had in my own life. I was the reason for my success. I had control, and I could make amazing things happen.

Once I rebuilt that self-worth, the next step was trusting myself. I needed to trust that I had the skills and the drive to make great things happen in my business. Trust in myself meant my self-worth was sustainable. Sustainable change is the only real change. I know that I've set myself up for success. Today, I can trust that even when things don't go according to plan, I have the resourcefulness to get back on track.

One of the best things I learned to do in my role as a corporate leader was to create amazing support systems. I recognized it was time to build my new support system, with an inner circle who I could spill my guts to and an outer circle of people who get me, who know what I'm creating and who do whatever they can to give me a leg up.

I've become my own biggest cheerleader. I know that I have to be my own biggest fan. It's become easier to fill that role when I acknowledge that what I have achieved didn't happen by accident, but because I put in the work.

Today, I can show up for my business, totally at peace, knowing who I am. Every coach I worked with helped me build a different piece of myself as I recovered from the very real trauma of losing my identity. It's not the kind of wound you can put a Band-Aid on.

Now I can see who I was when I lost my job and my identity. I was stressed out, maxed out and put all my eggs in the corporate basket. I didn't realize how much chaos I'd created. I didn't know that it was all connected. Once I took back control of my career, I had agency over my self-worth and my value. From there, I was able to create a serene state of mind and gain the energy I needed to grow my business, raise my family and still have time for myself.

Entrepreneurship isn't the only path to flexing that control. As I continue to pour my passion into my coaching business, I've also found a job I love. I choose to dedicate myself to this job during working hours and on my terms. It's giving me exactly what I need: stability to continue to make my dream of a stellar life into a reality.

Everything I went through to get to this place motivates me in my business. I don't want anyone else to have to go through that kind of debilitating period of identity loss and lack of control. I'm finally in complete alignment with what I'm doing, and I live the message that I bring to my clients.

The journey isn't over. No way. I'm so driven to get to the next level that I can be a bit impatient along the way. Sometimes I'm curious about whether I'm really making the right decisions. There are days when frustration wins out over optimism, but I don't get stuck in that place anymore. I know how to keep moving.

Heather Andrews isn't a job title. I stand for the opportunity to live a better life. I am all about integrity, self-respect and finding value in one's self. I know who I am and I'm fully at peace with Heather.

"The two most important days in your life are the day you are born and the day you find out why." —Unknown

Carrie-Ann Baron

Carrie-Ann helps individuals "Get real" so they can overcome tough obstacles and achieve personal and professional success. She has created her own s.o.u.l success formula through her versatile insights, and the works of many acknowledged spiritual and success teachers.

Carrie-Ann's journey of self-development, and having interviewed over a hundred experts on motivation and success around the globe, have helped her become a person that will be an asset to your personal, professional and spiritual growth.

She helps you see why your purpose is bigger than your objections. With her holistic approach to the elements that shape your victory, she is a key figure in your road to success and happiness.

Find Carrie-Ann online:

office@tenaciousliving.org
www.tenaciousliving.org
www.tlrstation.com

Chapter 2

Focus on Your Capabilities, not Your Limitations

By Carrie-Ann Baron

The day my whole world came crashing down around me, I had to do the complete opposite of what I'd been taught. I had to unreservedly, and lovingly take care of myself. I had to be the one in charge of my life.

My upbringing was all about taking care of others. It's no wonder I grew up a caring and compassionate person. I felt deeply and intuitively. Around age eleven or twelve, I thought I'd make a great psychologist, social worker, or therapist. I dreamed of studying abroad, seeing the world, and helping people.

Then I heard this from a beloved family member, "You're a care bear and always will be," she said. "You take on other people's problems as your own; you're always thinking of them to the point that you make yourself sick over it. It wouldn't be good for you to do that kind of job."

I was a kid, so I took her at her word. That was the start of decades of allowing other people to diagnose me and dictate how I should take care of myself. I was never comfortable in my skin. I repressed my feelings and built a life based on my parents' view of the world. They did it out of love. For me, though, the outcome wasn't a life I loved, rather one that I didn't recognize.

In my teens, I acquired another outsider's diagnosis. With the start of my period came fatigue, grogginess, and migraines. As if high school wasn't stressful enough, I started experiencing numbness and tingling in my hand and loss of coordination in gym class around my period. A doctor told me it was stress related and that I was overly sensitive. I took it to heart and became the stressed out, anxious girl who suffered silently every month while appearing active and happy; as if I knew exactly what I wanted.

By twenty-five, the numbness and tingling progressed significantly. The right side of my body often shook so bad that I woke up in the night dizzy and gasping for air. A doctor diagnosed me as epileptic, and I took on the identity willingly. I was prescribed anti-anxiety and anti-seizure medication. Those pills took a toll on my body, messing with my cycle, my kidneys, and my self-esteem.

Epilepsy became the reason for the way I was; my excuse when life didn't go according to plan. That didn't bring me any peace, though. I never felt relaxed or confident.

At the age of thirty-two, I reached a peak in my career. Work had become as much a part of my identity as epilepsy. I felt lost and stuck, and when I met a man online, I made the drastic decision to move halfway across the country to be with him.

My parents had guided my early life, and I let my job dictate my adult life. When I left my job to be with this guy, I left my identity behind too. I guess I thought if my life changed, my health might improve. I was right in a way, but I didn't know I was headed for rock bottom before any positive change could happen. Cue the tailspin.

Long story short: my epilepsy seemed to be in check, so I went off the medication. Within six weeks, I was diagnosed with erythema nodosum, an incredibly painful swelling underneath the skin on my shins. Things snowballed: between PMS and my period, I was hobbled most of the month. I suffered from insomnia and respiratory issues. My shin pain became chronic, and my shaking and seizures returned. On the rare occasions I did sleep, I was grinding my teeth hard enough to cause serious dental issues.

I consider myself an athletic person. I love to walk for hours at a time. When my symptoms stole my active life from me, I felt betrayed. It was as if my body wasn't my own (I gained a significant amount of weight), just like the rest of my life.

Shortly after moving to the new city, it became very apparent that he was not the guy I thought he was. He didn't want anything to do with me, so the relationship ended. I barely wanted anything to do with me. I needed to make a serious change immediately or risk throwing away the rest of my life.

If you'd asked me at the time what self-love meant, I probably would have told you it was selfish. "Putting yourself first? You must be a total narcissist." Over the course of several years, I would rebuild my entire worldview around self-love, self-care, and gratitude.

I started by focusing on my capabilities instead of my limitations. My constellation of symptoms meant that I was capable of watching television. So I did that. I watched a reality show profiling women who were making significant changes with the help of life coaches. Once, when the credits rolled by, I saw contact information for the coaches. Something stirred in me. I emailed a coach. It was a big step. I was making a statement that I was ready to invest time and money in myself. I didn't know it, but this action to support myself was self-love in action.

My new coach asked me about my intentions. "I want to feel comfortable in my skin," I told her, trying to remember if I'd ever felt like myself. She saw that I was overwhelmed, lost, confused, and angry. In fact, so much anger came out of me that my workplace asked me to attend anger management counseling.

My counselor helped me to realize that I was in love with a man who didn't love me the way I needed him to; and this was the trigger for the underlying anger. It was festering inside me. I needed to learn to love myself.

This was a different kind of diagnosis. It wasn't something that would define me. I would need to learn what it meant to love myself. That was scary.

I realized that this was about more than just loving me for me. It also meant listening to my body to learn how to deal with my seemingly insurmountable health issues that had been my identity, my excuse, and my reality.

My mission was clear: I needed to learn to enjoy life within the limitations of my body.

I was tiptoeing my way into self-love when I got a new family doctor. He suggested I build habits to address my symptoms one by one so that I didn't become overwhelmed by the enormity of it all. At my worst, I only felt 'normal' one day a month. I was often bedridden, on a restrictive diet, and unable to go out in the sunshine. We had to take things very slowly.

One of the first things I discovered with my doctor was that I never had epilepsy. It was a misdiagnosis, and I had been taking unnecessary medication for years. My shaking symptoms were likely a manifestation of an untreated panic and anxiety disorder that also resulted in obsessive and addictive tendencies.

I was referred to a psychiatrist who made the most brilliant statement. "Carrie-Ann, you are not your diagnosis. Your social phobia and anxiety is not your personality," he told me.

The weight of the world lifted off my shoulders at that moment. I'd always felt like a disappointment to everyone in my life. I didn't understand why I reacted to the world the way I did when inside I didn't feel like that anxious, panicked person. When I realized that my body was hijacked by my disorder and that it wasn't truly me, I felt like I could forgive myself. I didn't have to feel guilty, confused or angry anymore. Most importantly, it meant that change was possible, and I could be the one to make it.

I began to learn about neuro-linguistic programming, metaphysical and holistic healing, yoga, meditation and chakra alignment. I was working on healing my soul, my connection to God, the Universe, and my humanity.

I continued to work through my symptoms. After a few painful dead-ends with one gynecologist, I saw another who sent me to get a series of ultrasounds. The results came back. My family doctor called me in and told me that I had fibroid cysts in my uterus, and they were growing fast. I asked what that meant.

"How attached are you to your uterus?" he asked. I burst into tears. I'd never thought much about my uterus before. Who does until something is wrong with it? I went home, angry at the world.

I was curled up on my couch, cursing the world and everyone in it, when there was a knock on my door. Something told me I needed to answer it. I wrote a poem about what happened next.

Alone in my home

focusing on the task at hand

A knock on the door

who could it be?

Looking through the peep hole

I see my neighbor

she has two cups of hot apple cider

and some treats on a tray

I open the door

Understanding why she came over

We sit in the living room

Sipping on apple cider

She listens to me rant

She listens while I try to make sense of it all

Obstacles Equal Opportunities

She is here for support and

She even laughed at my attempts at humor

She said it is okay to be mad,

It is okay to be sad

It is even okay to be calm.

Knowledge, understanding, and Wisdom are the keys

The unexpected kindness of others

is what keeps the spirit of hope, the spirit of peace

and the spirit of love alive.

My neighbor helped me see what I couldn't. This momentous health discovery was an opportunity, not a limitation.

The gynecologist gave me three options for dealing with my uterus. Two would be temporary fixes. A third was permanent.

The doctor made it perfectly clear. "You can continue to go through this pain every month for the next twenty or thirty years, or you can have a hysterectomy, heal fast because you're young, and then enjoy the rest of your life healthy and pain-free." She explained that while I might be able to conceive in my current state, it would likely be a difficult pregnancy.

I took a week to think. I had struggled with crippling health issues my entire adult life, and now I knew so much of it stemmed from my rogue uterus. My instinct was that it was selfish to have surgery. I'd be denying my parents the chance to have grandkids, and a future, unknown partner the chance to have our biological kids.

At the same time, I saw the Universe was providing me with an opportunity to repair my health and restore my authentic self. Of course, I had to take this step. I saw a healthy future for myself, where I was living life instead of letting it pass me by. I found myself immensely grateful despite what might have looked from the outside to be dire.

I wanted my life back. I wanted to wake up feeling healthy and to move again. I told my doctor, "Let's do this!" To ease recovery, she suggested I start exercising and build up my strength in the six months leading up to the surgery.

I began with small acts of courage that respected my limits while nurturing myself physically and mentally. I took walks on my lunch break, browsing a nearby store, then journaling about what I appreciated about it, like a breeze blowing through my hair. I took drives toward the mountains. I had the energy to drive for twenty minutes. I'd pull over, read a bit of an inspirational book, and then drive home. When I felt stronger, I explored new routes, but always with a backup plan in case of emergencies.

I rediscovered myself while valuing myself, and always respected my body's capabilities. I was true to myself while being determined to succeed.

Surgery went well, and I committed myself to recovery, which required grieving my losses. I gave myself permission to grieve the loss of my uterus, my fertility, making my parents grandparents, making my sister an auntie, and so much more. I knew it was important to move through those feelings, but not dwell on them.

When recovery from surgery was done and I had the green light to resume living, I decided that to embrace the person who has always been inside. It was time to rediscover who I truly was.

I took bigger steps of courage. I joined a triathlon training group. At first, putting on my running shoes was as far as I'd get. Some days I would just make it out the front door to feel the sunshine on my face, and I was grateful.

Within three months, I was swimming, learning to run and cycling. In twelve weeks, I was active at least thirty minutes a day, five days a week. I remembered that at my worst, I'd had to crawl to the bathroom, crying in pain, and now here I was, training for a triathlon.

When one of the women in my triathlon training group asked if anyone would consider doing the IronMan in three years, I gave an enthusiastic, "Yes!" The IronMan is a 2.4-mile swim, a 112-mile bike ride, and a marathon 26.2-mile run. I wanted to live life, not just have a life. As I committed myself to training over the next three years, I stayed invested in my intention, while releasing myself from the outcome.

On August 26, 2012, I heard these words: "Carrie-Ann, you are an IronMan!" I crossed the finish line in 16 hours, 52 minutes and 10 seconds.

To cross that finish line, I had to learn how to love myself, how to respect my body and in that process, I discovered my purpose. I had to become the compassionate, caring, and intelligent woman I knew I was meant to be. I was finally awake to the infinite possibilities available to me and within me.

Since then, I've dedicated myself to building a business focused on helping, always with an underlying commitment to self-love. I call it Tenacious Living. My organization is founded on the belief that one person can make the difference and it starts with taking care of yourself. My mission is to support others to be true to themselves, keep their commitments to themselves and use their determination for themselves.

What started as a private life coaching practice has grown into a multifaceted company. It includes mentoring holistic practitioners one on one to elevate their healing practices, founding a podcast network for alternative and holistic health solutions, hosting a global telesummit called Escaping Emotional Chaos. I've even compiled a book of twenty-nine true short stories called Tenacious Living: Choosing Your Adventure.

I continue to focus on the good and nurture myself every single day. Faced with the option of being a victim of my circumstances or focusing on what I am capable of doing, I choose the latter.

I know now I'm the only one who can define my life.

Sarah Barrett

Sarah is a lively entrepreneur who's building an exciting career in social commerce. After graduating with a degree in business and entrepreneurship, she enjoyed a successful career in special event management. Faced with serious medical illness, Sarah forged a path through conventional approaches and redefined wellness for herself and family. She overcame this obstacle and experienced the immense benefits of clean living.

Sarah is passionate about sharing what she has learned; her focus is now on wellness and health education. She enjoys teaching others about clean living, home detoxification, nutrition and the powerful use of essential oils. She believes that knowledge empowers people to take an active role in achieving their optimal health.

In her free time, Sarah can be found writing, enjoying her love of travel, fitness, and nutrition, or exploring the outdoors with her husband and two boys.

Find Sarah online:

https://www.facebook.com/oilygal.yl
oilygal.yl@gmail.com
www.instagram.com/oily_gal

Chapter 3

The Powerful Gifts of Grit

By Sarah Barrett

"You don't drown by falling in the water. You drown by staying there."

- Edwin Cole Lewis.

Ten years ago, I was in love with my life. As an ambitious type-A personality, I believed that if you worked hard, you could have the life you want. I bought into this early on and clung to it in a rudimentary way. I was well on my way to creating the life of my dreams. I was proud of my accomplishments; full of passion— with my goals organized and was always ready to embark on the next adventure. It honestly hadn't occurred to me that my life could take many unexpected turns.

I had experienced substantial adversity in my life, and that introduced me to the concept of 'grit.' Grit is what we earn as we pass through challenges. The process of becoming gritty is messy and unstructured. It's the reward for enduring our suffering and

29

growing because of it. I found that adversity can carry with it many gifts — if we're receptive.

My parents divorced in my early teens, and I thought I knew it all, so I rebelled. I made choices that carried life-long impacts for many people. Faced with adult decisions at age fifteen, I learned profound lessons of loss and love. I gained the gift of unwavering faith by developing an infinite trust that the situation would turn out for the best. Faith has carried me through the worst of days. In my later teens, I survived a long, dark dance with the cunning eating disorder– bulimia. To overcome it I learned the value of nutrition and began living a healthier lifestyle. Exercise became a trusted friend, and I welcomed the gift of resilience.

By the time I was thirty, I'd graduated with a degree in business and entrepreneurship and was well into building an exciting career in event management. My fiancé and I had a blossoming relationship, and I was a new mother to an amazing one-year-old son. We had settled into our first home and were busy creating our lives together.

In the distance, an ugly black storm was brewing. The next decade would bring a series of stressful events, shattering my reality and relentlessly building my grit.

Six weeks before my wedding I was on my way to meet the florist when I received the phone call that changed my life. It was from the hospital social worker; there had been an incident with my father. A concrete-like dread filled my body.

I raced into the emergency room, pleading for someone to help me. I was sitting on a cold bench when a paramedic asked if he could help. My heart was heavy with intuition as I uttered my father's name. The paramedic's eyes confirmed what I already knew. My father, my best friend, had passed away from a major heart attack at the age of fifty-seven. I didn't get to say goodbye. The air left my lungs with the tight squeeze of shock. It was a long time before breathing became comfortable again.

Somehow, only because of divine grace, I had strength to organize his memorial service and continue with our wedding. My heart was shattered. I spent that first year feeling as if someone had blasted a hole in my chest with a shotgun. Grief, loss, and trauma don't come with a timeline. I learned I am a highly sensitive person who feels things very deeply. Each time I thought relief was coming, I was smashed with another wave of anguish; it was impossible to predict.

My husband's career took him away from home most of the year, and I found myself alone. I was still adjusting to life without my father, but the shock and numbness were wearing off. To see myself through I had again relied heavily on my exercise routines, and had also discovered yoga and meditation. These became tools to manage emotion and facilitate healing. I believed the joy in my life would return. Like a new bud reaching for sunlight after winter, I was beginning to live again.

In 2010, we welcomed a beautiful, healthy baby boy. I was overcome with love and pure joy as we became a family of four.

Then, another storm smashed in.

Overnight, my body became a stranger to me. I was blindsided with unexplained neurological symptoms. I would lose my balance and fall over unexpectedly. Without warning, my vision would become unfocused. Sunlight became unbearable. Every noise was amplified, and intense migraines were a daily occurrence.

Day after day the symptoms continued. For the next three years I developed a web of complicated, seemingly unrelated symptoms:

gastrointestinal problems, heart rhythm changes (including a heart block), joint pain, muscle spasms and weakness, air hunger, head pressure, autonomic dysfunction, raging insomnia, crippling fatigue, memory loss and cognitive decline, anxiety, low body temperature, hypoglycemia, and hormonal imbalances. The list felt endless.

I spent the first years of my new baby's life with my body taken hostage in a medical horror show.

My life became a host of emergency room visits; I was frantic for answers. My new normal consisted of appointments and testing with multiple specialists. On any given day, I experienced up to fifty symptoms. The inside of the doctor's office became my children's playground.

Unable to find a cause for my deteriorating body, I was stuck. I had gone from excellent physical condition to being so weak that being able to get out of bed and shower was a good day. My body could no longer do what I needed it to.

I was becoming unable to care for my children. On one trip to the emergency room, I was hooked to monitors as my heart rate was plummeting again. Electrophysiology had been called in for a consult. I fought with all of my might to push aside thoughts of dying. I couldn't leave my tiny babies.

The terror and uncertainty were crippling. I would lie awake at night begging for morning to bring reprieve.

Navigating our medical system isn't something a thirty-something-year-old dreams of. I was lost in a medical nightmare. I floundered for answers while being fully aware of the whispers behind my back. Many people were skeptical—including medical professionals. They didn't believe I was physically ill, but I knew my body was failing me. My resolve to live became stronger.

Three exhausting years after my first symptom, a doctor diagnosed 'it.' The mysterious monster had a name: late-stage neurological Lyme disease. I was so relieved to have an answer. Now I could fight back!

However, after some research, I realized my journey had just begun. Neurological Lyme disease is extremely challenging to treat. It's one of the most politically charged and controversial diseases in modern history. Proper care and testing for this condition are not available in Canada. Think AIDS patients during the 1980s. Lyme sufferers are shamed into silence by ignorance and outdated diagnostics. There is an extreme lack of funding for research and treatment is complicated and inaccessible.

Lyme disease is unpredictable. Like a thief in the night, it robs the familiar—slowly, like a river eroding a bank; life, as I knew it was gone.

I didn't recognize my own face. I had become a broken, vacant shell of myself. Living daily with a disease no one understands is incredibly isolating and corrosive to relationships. Lyme disease sufferers bear the crushing burden of shame and rejection in the medical system. It became awkward to talk about and I sunk deeper into isolation.

The questions whirled in my mind leaving traces of fear and desperation in their wake. Would it ever end? How was I going to make it through this? It was humbling.

This disease stripped my life down to the most basic functions. Using my energy for anything other than survival was impossible. I had only one hope: to get better. I didn't know anyone with this disease. I had to forge my path through the darkness. Step. By step. By step.

In the beginning, I wasted precious time coveting the lives of my peers. They were out doing regular mom activities and building their careers while I was struggling to reclaim my body. I was so resistant toward my experience that it was impossible for things to change.

Acceptance of my reality was challenging but necessary. This was a new concept for me. I was used to 'doing' to get out of situations. I got brave and brutally honest about where I currently was. Acceptance. I was learning another gift.

Through the minutes, hours and days, I earned the gritty gifts of perseverance and tenacity. I trusted that any movement would initiate change. So I began moving.

Practicing meditation and mindfulness became a core activity to my healing, as I couldn't exercise. I learned how to sit and be still in the fire of my circumstance. Being in these raw, sometimes terrifying moments created important transformations in my perception. I learned to identify emotions and communicate with my body. I experienced the gift of release, and how to surrender the things I had no control over to foster receptiveness and peace. I learned how to respect my limits and trust the process. I had to let go of my ideals, opinions, expectations and judgments, as well as those of others. I had to allow things to be as they were.

The space created by mindfulness practice was the gateway for most of the changes that would happen for me. I learned that authentic living required me to re-align with my core values. I moved toward heart-centered and mindful living. I cultivated intentional focus and gratitude to notice things that resonated with me and released the things that did not.

I learned we have to be ok with the chaos, stress, and the unknown. I didn't know how the situation would turn out, so I had to create enough space to be able to breathe while in it. Acceptance doesn't mean we are stuck there; rather, it offers an opportunity to change.

I was still extremely sick, but my experiences began to change despite my circumstances remaining the same. When I was able to deconstruct and peel away the unnecessary in my life, the gift of intuition was fortified. I started unapologetically owning my story and I followed my instincts. A powerful transformation occurred. I had to rebuild and move forward with instinct as my compass.

I dove into research about health and wellness with fresh eyes. What I found was a reactive and backward system. Our healthcare is often sick care. Prevention of disease rarely gets consideration. We have a symptom and go to the doctor. Then the doctor prescribes medication, sometimes with potentially harmful side effects.

I chose to follow a natural path back to wellness—considering my body in its entirety. I am blessed; our family could afford to send me to a world-renowned physician who specialized in the treatment of complex diseases by utilizing this approach.

The nights were still grueling and the days relentless. I would make progress and then encounter brutal setbacks. I underwent procedures, some of which were excruciating. I learned how to adapt, and using the gift of awareness; I resigned myself to notice and cultivate the good around me, no matter how bad it seemed. Being isolated in so many capacities gave me an opportunity to reflect on my life and offered the chance to rebuild it. Piece by piece, I began picking up the fragments of my broken self.

I spoke my truth and learned the twin gifts of vulnerability and courage. As a result, I received the gift of connection. I began having honest conversations with other patients while sitting in clinic treatments. I heard their stories. I allowed my story to be heard. I looked for opportunities to serve those around me who were also suffering. Often, no words were needed; the power of the connection transcended language. These connections brought new meaning to my experiences.

Passing through tragedy introduced me to the gifts of empathy and compassion. Being able to offer support for others is an immense blessing. My path has merged with incredible people because of this illness, and I understand the transformative potential of holding space and witnessing another person's experience. I have built a powerful tribe of like-minded, supportive individuals.

I also learned to connect with myself through the art of radical self-compassion and care. I had to make healing a priority. I learned to say no and set boundaries to prevent things that drained my energy. I practiced being in the moment, noticing the beauty in each breath I took.

I learned to be gentle and love myself, and to appreciate who I still was, raw, broken and imperfect. I learned to release my patterns of negative self-talk and empty ideals.

I realized I wasn't defined by my achievements, things that happened to me, or mistakes I made. I cultivated the gift of gratitude. By being consciously grateful for tiny things, the joy in my life was amplified, even in the midst of my suffering.

I began to honor the delicate balance between the rest I needed for healing and the connection I also needed from being of service to others. Both were essential.

This illness has tested and expanded my physical and mental boundaries. I have faced many temporary moments of defeat. I've spent nights in solitude when my broken body wept, and I wanted to give up. I know what it feels like to shake violently with fear of death and the unknown.

Self-discipline and a clear vision (eliminating the distractions and the unnecessary) are valuable tools for rebuilding a life. Through daily activity and consistent follow through, I have reconstructed my life. I applied this consistency and resolve to my treatment, to slowly getting my strength back through exercise, to daily nutrition and adequate rest.

We may not have any control over some of the events in our lives, but we have control over our response. We can reframe our experiences and create meaning from our suffering. To quote the brilliant author and shame researcher, Brené Brown, "We can write our own daring endings." I am a survivor, and I choose to be a light for others.

My adversities have revealed my biggest blessings. My experience introduced me to social causes I am now an advocate for. Lyme disease treatment and diagnosis in Canada needs to be reformed.

Empowered by the changes I was seeing in my family, and myself, I knew my approach worked. I devoured information on nutrition, chemical-free living, and supporting the body with natural alternatives. By integrating this knowledge, I have been able to forge a path to recovery that has bought me a new lease on life. This has led me to embark on a new career path. I'm passionate about sharing the benefits of a lifestyle free from harsh chemicals and helping others to make positive changes in their lives.

In the awkward space of transition, where you don't belong to your past and don't know your future, there is space. Pause there and investigate. Get curious even though it may be uncomfortable. Be open to receiving.

Grit is earned in the trenches of experience. Grit offers the opportunity to boldly learn things about ourselves we couldn't have learned otherwise. We are rewarded with its many gifts: faith, resilience, hope, perseverance, acceptance, release, intuition, awareness, vulnerability, courage, connection, empathy, compassion and gratitude. Respect and be patient with your experience. It is the greatest teacher of all.

"These pains you feel are messengers, listen to them."

- Rumi

Jamie Barton

Jamie is an entrepreneur, widower and most importantly—the father of an inspiring young boy. Through his wife Jill's journey with breast cancer, they were often faced with debilitating challenges. Realizing that there was only one way out, he listened to his wife's wishes and enacted change to make the community that he lives in stronger. His nine-year-old son Tate has successfully ran Tate's Lemonade Stand for three years, raising over $26,000 for their local cancer clinic.

Find Jamie online:

Facebook.com/tateslemonadestand

Chapter 4

When Life Leads You Down an Unexpected Road

By Jamie Barton

September 19th, 2013. I will never forget that day. The day my family's life changed forever. The day I added titles to my name I never planned on. I went from being a husband and father to a widower and a single father to my five-year-old son.

We knew what was coming, but we weren't prepared. Not really. Jill had done her best to make plans and record her wishes, but the reality of her finite life just hadn't sunk in.

My wife had been battling aggressive breast cancer for a long time. It took so much of her strength to make it that far. It would take months longer for me to see that all the challenges we had faced as a family, and the friends and strangers who made sure we got through it, would make Tate and me stronger, kinder people.

Before we lost Jill, we made memories. In mid-August, we had a date with the Tom Baker Cancer Center. These dates had become a regular thing. Since we live in the small town of High River, we treated these cancer consultations in the big city as a chance to embrace our time together and go on dinner dates. This particular trip, Jill wanted to visit a famous drive-in burger joint, and I eagerly agreed.

We took our food and ate at a picnic table, enjoying some of the simpler things in life: fresh air and nature. While we were digging into our burger and fries, Jill abruptly changed the discussion. In true Jill fashion, she delivered her message bluntly. This was not uncommon since her cancer diagnosis. I knew she was making plans for Tate and me, and that they weren't quite finished.

"Tate needs a woman in his life," Jill said. "He needs a mom."

It was weird to hear those words from Tate's mom, but I understood. She didn't want to leave her boy lacking anything in life. Then she continued. Jill told me I needed a woman in my life too.

With a lump in my throat, I realized the enormity of her words. She was saying it without saying it. Jill wasn't going to be here forever, and she was clearly giving us permission to carry on with life after she was gone.

As soon as she started the conversation, it was over. Back to burgers, French fries, and fresh air. Years later, I can appreciate the planning she did and the approach she took to spare us whatever pain she could. It was only a few sentences with the smell of deep fryers in the background, but it was so important. It was so Jill.

Early in her diagnosis, Jill and I decided to tell our young son what was happening. Little ears hear things, much of which we don't even realize until much later. We knew Tate would eventually start asking, "What is cancer?" and "what is happening?" We approached it the best way we knew, with honesty and clarity. It gave us one less thing to worry about as we moved forward. We needed to leverage any advantage to defend against this illness that had so much power over us.

We stuck to honesty with our friends and our small town community too. Jill wanted people to see what cancer does to a person and their family. I wonder if she could have imagined what an impact she would have on our community in the long-term. It made all the difference; she started us on a path to awareness and advocacy.

Jill was very active in our community. She golfed in the summers and curled in the winters. It seemed like she knew just about everyone. Every day at work, Jill lent her ear to clients, as hairdressers often do. She and her friends from a mommy group were always sharing stories when they got together to watch their kids play. She was connected.

When Jill's diagnosis became public, we began to learn what a true community could be.

In our time of need, our town's true colors bloomed. Everything from childcare to a stocked fridge and freezer made life a little easier. Our friends and neighbors helped us through many hard times.

Among these gifts of love, they granted Jill a wish she'd had since her diagnosis. Plans were in the making so she could experience the sun on the beaches of the Pacific and walk down Main Street at the happiest place on Earth while wearing a set of mouse ears with her son. That trip, a little more than a year before we lost Jill, was incredible. I will never forget it, and I'll always cherish it.

Shortly after we returned from the trip, Jill had a follow-up MRI scheduled with the hopes of figuring out why her legs were tingling and feeling numb during our trip. She never revealed these sensations to me while we were away, trying to shield me from more worry. The MRI was on a Friday morning, and we had plans to enjoy the late-summer day with a family barbecue later.

Everything at the MRI seemed routine, and the oncologist said he would call us about the results. Dinner had just started when the phone rang. More news that she didn't want to hear. Jill's breast cancer had infiltrated her spinal cord, and she would likely stop walking. Probably within days, we were told.

On Sunday, she woke up unable to move from the waist down. We were devastated. We all knew her fate, but we didn't expect this curveball. Immediately, we changed our lives and learned what it was like for a cancer fighter to be subjected to life in a wheelchair. This was our fall of 2012.

We struggled with disbelief but faced reality. We needed to accommodate Jill's abilities. The simplest of tasks now came with a completely different perspective. Our house needed to be accessible; we needed people around Jill at all times. We realized that life was not going to get easier.

This was when a lot of Jill's serious planning took place. She made it very clear that life would continue for Tate and me. She made me promise that we would show our community how much we appreciated their love and support. Jill wanted us to make a difference in our world. She was adamant that we advocate for health and promote prevention through education. If there was any way to avoid it, Jill wanted nobody else to go down the same path as she did.

From fall into spring 2013, we seemed to be continually renovating our home for accessibility. We installed hardwood flooring so Jill could navigate more easily. We widened doors and tried to predict any possible barriers before they got in Jill's way. Every week there was a new challenge, particularly as the cancer progressed. Then something hit that we couldn't predict.

June 19th, 2013 was a day no one in our town could ever forget.

The day started out pretty normal, although we were expecting fast-flowing waters to pass through town. The Highwood River often swelled in the spring then subsided quickly. No big deal. I made my way to work out of town in the early morning hours before the sun had made it up and before the water started to rise. That week my father-in-law, Joe, was staying with us. For months he helped us immensely, making sure Tate got to school and Jill was looked after.

Around 10 am, he called me. He wanted to ease my mind about the water flow. He told me not to get too excited about the raging river. There was some water flowing down the curbs, but that was about it.

Within minutes of us hanging up the phone, the river breached a dike. Water rushed into town and toward our house.

I heard the news reports and tried to phone home. I pictured Jill at home in her wheelchair and Tate playing with his school friend, unaware. I tried to call, but all telephone communications were taken out by the high water. I had no idea if they had a plan to get out or where they would go once they did. I left work in a panic.

By the time I got close to town, the radio station news reports were calling the flooding an unprecedented event. Water had reached every part of town, and all the available information led me to believe our house would be underwater. My mind wandered to places I never wanted it to go. The very real possibility became clear: I may never see my family again, and there was nothing I could do.

I managed to get to within a few blocks of our home. Water had risen to six feet deep in places. I still had no idea where my family was. I was approached by emergency responders who asked me to retreat to higher ground immediately. I reluctantly agreed, trying to push grim thoughts from my mind, frustrated that all I could do was wait and hope.

That wasn't good enough, I decided. I made my way to an emergency command center and enlisted the help of the emergency response personnel. I explained the situation, and they quickly made a plan to get to our home.

Eventually, I could breathe again. Within an hour of my arrival in town, everyone who had been in our house made it out. Barely. The rescue vehicle carrying my family and my son's friend had just crossed the last bridge back to the emergency command center before it was violently washed out. It was like a scripted scene in a movie. It couldn't have been closer. Someone was watching over them that day. I cried. I was never so happy to see my loved ones.

Along with the other thirteen thousand residents of High River, we had to scramble for a place to live. It had to be a place that could accommodate Jill and her wheelchair. It was daunting.

We landed at my in-laws on their acreage in the town of Okotoks, about 25 km north of where the river had likely flooded whatever was left of our worldly possessions. They welcomed us with open arms, and we started to figure out our next family move.

On July 1st, we were able to see what was left of our home. It was surreal. What had started as just another spring day turned out to be the largest natural disaster in Canada at the time.

I felt numb as I looked at our flooded home. Each new punch life threw at us had now become unbearable. I had no idea how our town was going to get through this, but I knew we just had to start to rebuild our lives.

The day after we saw our home, a neighbor came by to talk about a plan for cleanup. Some of his friends offered to help both of our families the next day. This was encouraging. The plan was for about ten people to offer their help and I was extremely grateful.

The next morning, when my in-laws and I arrived at our house, they expected to see around ten people. There were sixty-three people there. These sixty-three people voluntarily cleared mud, water, ruined furniture and keepsakes out of our house. People I'd never met had come to help. I was overcome with emotion.

I saw first-hand what 'community' was all about, and I was never prouder to be a Higher Riverite. It was heart-wrenching to watch strangers mucking out my home. It was like living through an episode of an extreme home makeover show. They cleaned our entire basement within three-and-half-hours.

One month later, many had worked their butts off to make sure my wife could see her home again and live in some peace. At this point in her journey, she was failing before my eyes. I'm so grateful she was able to be in our home again. The community lifted us up, and I will forever be in debt to them all.

On September 19th, Jill succumbed to the effects of breast cancer. It had spread to many regions of the body, and ultimately, to her brain.

I still miss her profoundly. I miss her dreams. I miss her presence. I miss her.

Early the next spring, when our son had turned six, he asked his uncle Joe how he could make some money. Joe gave him economics 101: how to run a lemonade stand. I still have a photo of Tate from this day, and I treasure it. When I took it, I didn't know what was coming next. It was the day my son and our family began to give back to our community. We were on the path Jill had wanted us to find: a path to recovery.

Later in the spring, Tate wanted to raise some funds in memory of his mother. He hoped to donate about $100 to our small community cancer clinic, which had looked after his mom. We needed a venue to facilitate his latest lemonade endeavor, and we found it in our community's annual Little Britches Parade.

I didn't want him to be disappointed, so I tucked five twenty-dollar in my pocket in the event his lemonade sales didn't meet his goal.

Tate raised $3,800 that day.

Now, after three years, Tate has managed to raise over $26,000 to help High River Cancer Clinic. He's now nine and embarking on his fourth year of fundraising and is learning all about what it's like to give back to the very people that helped us out through our challenges.

I have never been more proud of him. I know his mother is always looking down on him, guiding him along this path. All of Jill's plans are underway.

Through this journey, I have also learned how I can support people as they travel down the path of cancer. My hope is to cast some light on what is ahead, especially for the kids and husbands involved. I know I found it helpful to talk with others who had been down the same path. Giving back is now part of my life's role.

I am a single father of a nine-year-old boy. My life has changed in ways I never would have imagined, but we are stronger for all the adversities we have faced. I know the past will get us through the next set of challenges.

I hope my son and I can continue to advocate for health and our community. I am forever grateful for everyone who helped us along the way. My life is richer for being able to repay their generosity.

This is my story, but it's really about my wife and our son, the two people who changed my life. They are my heroes.

Sara Bell

Sara left her day job to care for her nana with Alzheimer's, while pursuing her dream of entrepreneurship. She created a service-based company offering support to businesses who don't have teams to dedicate to the customer experience.

Sara leads by example and made it her mission to enhance experiences by supporting the growth and relationships of her clients and their teams. She wholeheartedly believes that even if your path is unconventional, everyone has something to contribute, and by actively cultivating relationships (starting with the one with yourself!), you can achieve success beyond your wildest imagination.

Find Sara online:

sara@eventplanningsupport.com

Chapter 5

Finding Myself Through Loss

By Sara Bell

Just when I thought I was getting the hang of life, my world came crashing down around me. I lost my marriage, my grandfather, and my job within a few weeks of one another. It was October 2015, and my life was nothing like I imagined.

Marriage is a funny thing. It can look like someone has it together—two happy people in love and working toward a common goal. However, it can change suddenly and drastically. I knew we had challenges, but I thought we were making progress and working through them. It felt like he changed his mind overnight—and just like that—he was gone. My bank accounts were drained, and my credit cards were maxed out. My credit score was worse than ever. I was left with both cars and all the bills when he disappeared. He made me feel like it was my fault for months until the truth finally caught up with him. I was devastated, to say the least.

I spent a few months trying to keep myself busy so that I wouldn't have to think about it. It wasn't hard considering I needed to get two additional part-time jobs just to keep up with our expenses. I worked my full-time day job, drove for Uber in the evenings and weekends, and took a part-time job at a yoga studio in exchange for regular classes (since I could no longer afford them but needed desperately to escape from myself occasionally).

Any spare time I found, I slept. I didn't want to think, and the only way I could slow my mind was to sleep. Money started to seem scarcer, and as life would have it, I faced a company buyout. At first, I was told I would likely be kept for at least six more months (no guarantees, of course), but then I was presented with severance paperwork or a voluntary transfer to an entry level position back where I came from, almost a decade ago.

Desperate, and with new knowledge of my papa's lung cancer diagnosis, I took the transfer back home to San Diego. I tried to stay positive—I'm known for being pretty optimistic. Gradually, I felt more and more defeated. I was tired of smiling through it. Tired of trying to shine the shit. Tired of thinking and being positive.

I needed a change. I wanted to start over. I wanted to do the things I always wished I could do but never tried for one reason or another. The last straw came after I needed time off for my papa's funeral. I was told I could take it and would be supported. Later I found myself having to get my shift covered, not being able to take more than two days off to go to the funeral and grieve, and not receiving the full bereavement pay I was qualified to receive. It solidified my decision to quit almost overnight.

My nana was seventy-nine-years-old at the time, and my papa was her caregiver. When he passed, I knew she needed someone to care for her full-time, and I felt in my heart that I should be that person. I also knew I could create my version of success and happiness by working for myself, so I asked my parents and uncles if they would help support me (by paying for my cars, rent, food, clothes, and more). In return, I would help them by caring for her as long as possible, at least until her house sold so she could shift to a long-term living arrangement. I would start paying everything on my own as soon as I could. They agreed, even though it would be hard for all of us. I burned through what little I had saved to stay afloat during the first month.

I knew I would still need an income. My family would help with basic living expenses, but I still had extra bills to pay. I still needed money in the bank to pay for lingering issues after my divorce. I faced a civil suit from my soon to be ex-husband and knew that it could cost me even more. I needed to maintain my independence—the last thing I wanted to do was go from being a divorcee to being dependent on my family for everything. I decided I would take my experience and go to work for myself in whatever spare time I found. Owning my own business had always been a dream—I could finally turn it into reality, albeit via a less than conventional route.

I soon realized it would be easier said than done, but I was determined to make it work. Caring for my nana was more than a full-time job. We were attached at the hip. I did everything with her. I mean everything. We ate together, slept together, showered together—you name it, I had to do it with her. If I left her alone for a moment, she would be out the door or getting herself into trouble. With her level of Alzheimer's, everything is a hazard.

Alzheimer's is one of the shittiest things I've ever had to deal with, and while I'm great at sharing the happiest moments, I'm not immune to the downfalls of it. My nana has no idea who I am or why I'm relevant to her. She shares no memories with me. As long as she's entertained, she doesn't miss me or care about where I am, what I'm doing, or about anyone else for that matter. She is still here physically, though mentally she is long gone. She can have simple conversations, but she has a hard time expressing her true thoughts. I've spent the last year figuring out what works best for us in the moment, to maintain the peace in her otherwise chaotic and ever changing mind.

Every day for the past year, I woke up earlier than her to work on my laptop in bed. If I got out of bed, she would be behind me in a minute, so I had to stay there with her. I did the same in the wee hours of the night. Eventually, I got her into an adult day center program, which gave me a five to six hour break in the day during which I could work without distraction. This also gave me back my regular sleeping hours.

I quickly realized the dream of family/work/life balance is bullshit. Balance is bullshit. You have to integrate your work/business into your life and do what works for you. There are no quick paths to success. What works for others may not work for you, and that's ok. You have to find your own way.

I started my business focused on what made me money instantly, and surprise, I hated it! I was doing the exact things I hated in my previous corporate jobs (virtually assisting with tasks for less money than I felt it deserved).

That's when I learned about pivoting. There was a brief moment when I thought I failed, but I couldn't turn back—I committed to caring for nana for as long as possible, and couldn't go back to a 'normal' job, even if I wanted to. Therefore, this time, I was fully committed.

What the hell do you do when nothing seems to be working? You shift gears.

I started focusing on the things I liked and started saying no to things I hated or simply wasn't interested in. Does that mean I turned down money? Absolutely. Nevertheless, what happened next floored me—I gained two new clients and doubled my income while working less than before (and doing more of what lights me up!). A win? I think so!

It's not always perfect—clients pay late, I have more on my plate than I can handle at times, and I may go back to a corporate position sooner than I thought. However, this time around it is with a different perspective and less of a mapped out plan for myself!

Needless to say, the past two years have been a whirlwind.

Perhaps the biggest effect that processing all of this loss (my marriage, my papa, my nana's mind, my 'normal' life) has had on me, are the realizations about myself that I could never have learned without going through this.

As I approach thirty, I'm nowhere near where I thought I would be by now. My life has changed drastically, more than once. Alzheimer's is a progressive disease and knowing my nana would only get worse, I spent the past year knowing I was merely prepping her to live at a memory care facility. When she moved in there just a few short weeks ago, I felt a huge weight lift and simultaneously felt more drastic changes coming my way.

If there's one thing I know for sure, it's that your life is what you make it. I said that in a speech once, and I don't think I fully understood what it meant until now.

Life is a constant stream of choices. Some will be good, some bad—and some you'll wish you hadn't made at all. I always thought I was damned to a particular path until I finally let go of my endless life plans. I finally realized I needed to give myself permission to change my mind.

It's ok to change your mind; you are not damned to a specific path because you made a decision that didn't work out as you thought it would. Change directions. You know all you need to know to move forward. Trust yourself.

The world needs you—it needs you at your worst—and it needs you at your best. You are an integral part of our society whether you realize it or not. Sometimes when you're in the shit, it can seem hopeless. Being positive just isn't possible, and that's ok. You don't have to be put together and perfect all the time. Sometimes you have to dredge through the shit to get to the other side. Even then, life won't be perfect. However, you'll be better off for having handled your shit and learned even more about yourself than you ever thought possible.

Nicole Buck

Nicole has worked as a medical radiologic technologist since 2005, with additional education in psychology through Queen's University, and is also an entrepreneur in the health and wellness industry Arbonne International, since 2007.

Suffering from a major depression disorder, she has gone through a divorce, a traumatic emergency surgery, job loss and money troubles. She continues to fight, love and share with others on keeping a positive mindset while believing in yourself.

Nicole believes wholeheartedly in building people up and sharing in a vision for themselves that is bigger and bolder than what they could ever imagine.

Find Nicole online:

www.linkedin.com/in/nicole-buck-17620168
www.nicoleneal.arbonne.com
www.facebook.ca/nicole.buck.77
www.facebook.com/inspiredbythejourney

Chapter 6

Love What Is

By Nicole Buck

I grew up thinking children would be a certainty in my life. However, when I was thirty-three, that reality came crashing down around me. After suffering a full week of fever, migraines and severe pelvic pain, I decided to go to the urgent care clinic to find out what was going on. I am an x-ray technologist, which may lead you to believe that I would know better than to let my symptoms go on for that long but no—I think being a health care professional can be a recipe to make you terrible patient! The doctor at the clinic gave me a prescription for antibiotics, T3s and a requisition for a pelvic ultrasound. I went to work the next day and got my ultrasound done when a tech had time to fit me in. Working in diagnostic imaging has its perks. Sorry to all of you that have waited for your exam to be booked, but it's true. I continued with my workday until the radiologist came and said that we needed to talk. You know it's never good when someone says "We need to talk."

I walked into his office, and he said, "I don't think your antibiotics are going to be strong enough to fix this issue. I think you'll need IV antibiotics. I've called the hospital and talked to an OB/GYN, and he is expecting to see you."

Me, not entirely grasping the seriousness of my situation, asked if the doctor was waiting to see me right now because I had tickets to a hockey game right after work.

The radiologist looked at me with such a confused expression and said, "I guess you could go tomorrow but I talked to this specific OB/GYNE personally, he is very difficult to get in and see, and he is expecting you now."

Oh. I guess I should go now then, I thought. I let my co-workers know that I had to go to the hospital. The radiologist and I apologized for leaving them short staffed. I was under the impression that I was just going to see this highly sought after specialist to hear his opinion, get some IV antibiotics, and be on my way. I was still thinking that I would be going to the hockey game. Some of my co-workers were kind enough to ask if I wanted a ride to the hospital, but I gratefully declined. *I'm ok,* I thought, *I can do this.*

I'm not sure if it was because I was trying to convince myself that this was no big deal when I was declining the help but suddenly, my brain registered the situation as being a tremendous deal. I started to fall apart. Tears, shaking, fear. At that moment, the assistant supervisor came up to me and insisted she take me to the hospital, and I complied.

I contacted my boyfriend and asked him to meet me at the hospital. I arrived and registered, but I didn't even have time to sit down before the nurse called me. She brought me to an exam room in the therapy area, started an IV, and took some blood. The specialist finally came in to see me to get a more detailed history and let me know who would be taking my case. A different doctor came in after to do a pelvic exam and ask me more questions. By now, my boyfriend had arrived and was waiting patiently to be allowed into my exam room. He waited around with me, and a short time later, four doctors came into my room to give me some answers. I may have been in denial before, but there isn't any denying four doctors entering your room to give you results and their opinion.

"Get out," I told my boyfriend. "Get out!" I yelled again. He wasn't moving fast enough I guess. I looked at them, and they looked at me. "Nicole, we need to admit you and get you on intense IV therapy for at least forty-eight hours," one doctor told me. "You are a very sick girl."

Oh, is that all? I thought to myself. *I know I'm sick, I feel like crap.* "Does today count as day one?" I asked, having one last chance at being in denial. "Ugh, no" one doctor replied. With that, my room emptied and became quiet. I felt so alone.

A while later a nurse came back to hook me up to an antibiotic cocktail of some kind and had a porter ready to take me up to the unit. I asked the nurse if I could get a day pass so I could still go to the hockey game, but of course, the answer was no. Yes, people, I am that much of a hockey fan that I still tried to go to the game just minutes after being admitted to the hospital. Where there's a will, there's a way, right? I guess not this time. I sent my boyfriend to the game and let a friend use my ticket.

So there I was. A patient in the hospital. The first evening a doctor came by to get more history and to see how I was feeling. I told him that I've had bilateral hydrosalpinx (fluid in both fallopian tubes) and chronic pelvic inflammatory disease since I was seventeen-years-old. The week before my hospital visit, I had been treating my fever and migraine with T1s and two extra strength Advil, switching between them every four hours. Naturally, his next question was if I was having regular bowel movements as they are both hard on the system. I said that I probably wasn't going to the bathroom enough and he replied with suggestions to aid that. I could take a Colace tablet, insert a suppository, or have an enema. I piped up real quick and pointed right at him. "Heck No! I'm not falling for that one!" I said. That totally caught him off guard, and he chuckled. I mentioned that I was an x-ray technologist and knew what enemas are all about. "Ok, Colace it is," he laughed.

Days came and went. I got a roommate; she had a hysterectomy and left the next day. I had a fever, and my white blood cell count went down. The next day my fever went down, and my white blood cell count went back up. None of the antibiotics the doctors put me on worked. Every other day they changed their minds about what they wanted to do with me. After three days of taking laxatives, I waved my hands to the nurses and said, "No more!" I couldn't stop going to the bathroom now. I was on so much medication I needed to be checked for colitis difficile, which is incredibly contagious and would have been put in isolation if I tested positive. The results did come back negative—thank God. That one piece of good news was quickly overshadowed by people from Infectious Disease Control entering my room to ask some questions. They explained that sometimes TB can show up in fallopian tubes and that's what they thought was responsible for my infection. Since I had a pre-existing condition that caused a fluid buildup in my tubes, they became a perfect nesting ground for TB.

A week went by, and I asked what my white blood cell count needed to be before they started to worry about sepsis (blood poisoning) because things can go downhill (organs can fail) very quickly at that point. I was told that if my white blood cell count went to thirty, they would start to worry. I was at twenty-three. It didn't look good, and the worst was yet to come.

During the week, I called my parents to give them an update on my condition. No matter how old you are, you always want your parents around in this kind of situation. The next morning the doctor stopped by and told me my white blood cell count was twenty-seven. I needed emergency surgery that day. I called my mom and was hysterical. Within three hours, she was on a plane to get to me. An hour after she had arrived a porter came to take me to the operating room. I started to cry, uncontrollably. I even pulled the sheet over my head as I lay on the stretcher because I was so terrified. The stress, the pain, the lack of sleep, the devastation of knowing that my fallopian tubes are going to be removed, the definitive result of not having children naturally, and the overall fear of surgery itself came to a peak at that moment.

I arrived in the theater holding room at 8 pm and waited for my surgeon to come. She walked in and talked me through the surgery in an attempt to calm me down. "We are doing this laparoscopically so that you will have three small incisions on your tummy and one in your belly button." Through my tears, I told her that I dreamed two weeks ago that I would need surgery and that they would find something on my uterus. She assured me that everything would be ok, and they weren't expecting to find anything on my uterus or any significant scarring. She said the surgery should only take fifteen minutes.

I was moved into the operating suite at 9 pm. The anesthesiologist injected the anesthetic, and I was out within seconds. The surgeon couldn't have been more wrong about the time my surgery would take.

I remember someone shaking my shoulder and saying, "Nicole." I slowly opened my eyes and asked what time it was. Someone told me it was 1 am. I did the math. That was four hours! "My tummy is on fire," I said, before falling asleep again.

The surgeon came to speak to me during her morning rounds. "You were a trouble maker last night," she said, with a stressed look on her face. "When we got in there, there was a lot of scarring and inflammation that we didn't expect to see. We were able to remove your right fallopian tube without incident, but when we started with your left tube, it burst. We cleaned all the infection, but we discovered that the left tube was stuck to your bowel. We had to do a colonoscopy while we were removing that tube so we could take away as much of the fallopian tissue as possible without creating a whole in your bowel." That wasn't the whole story though. There was more. She continued, "We also saw that your uterus is stuck to your bladder. Unfortunately, when we were taking out the laparoscopic devices, we saw that your catheter bag filled with blood. We had to cut you open and pull out your bladder to repair the two-centimeter hole on the top and the one-centimeter hole on the bottom that occurred during the surgery. You'll need to keep the catheter in for ten days so your bladder can heal." We looked at my abdomen and saw three small incisions that she mentioned I would have, another one a little bit bigger that had a drainage tube in it, and then a large incision along my bikini line that had ten staples and Steri-Strips on it. I was also hooked up to morphine and on oxygen. No wonder I was in so much pain!

Over the next few days, I tried to walk with the help of my nurse, but the pain and nausea were so bad that I could only make it to the door of my room and back. I was throwing up so much that my potassium level dropped and that caused concern as potassium's major role is to keep the heart working properly.

Can you believe that over those two weeks I was so sick that I couldn't eat anything, but I still gained twenty pounds! "That's crap!" I shouted at my nurse. All in good fun of course. I did laugh, but still…

On one of my assisted walks, I was struggling with nausea when I noticed a new patient walking toward me. I was the longest resident in my unit, so I knew that this lady was new. She smiled while walking, talking and laughing with a friend. She looked happy. She didn't look sick at all except for the fact that she was bald. I knew what that meant. We were both on the OB/GYNE unit—she had cancer. I stopped walking and started to cry. My nurse asked me what the matter was, and I told her that obviously, that woman had cancer, and I was going to be ok. I stood back up and started walking again. Yes, there will always be someone who has a bigger problem than you, but that doesn't mean you should ignore what you are feeling. You need to honor those feelings. That lady was having a good day. I, on the other hand, was not.

Finally, after two long weeks, I was being discharged! Both of my parents stayed in town until I was home for a few days and comfortable enough to move around. I had to go home with my catheter in so I needed to set my alarm to wake me every three hours at night to empty it so it wouldn't leak. My mom slept in my bed with me just to make sure I would be ok. I could barely walk let alone get out of bed on my own; it was so painful. As I lay down to sleep on my first night back home, my mom opened my bedroom window just a little crack and tucked a towel around my catheter bag just in case, and I started to cry. My mom leaned over, "Are you ok honey? What's wrong?" she asked.

"Mom," I replied. "I can feel the air I am breathing. I can feel the fresh, clean air as I breathe." What a moment of gratitude.

I suffered from PTSD for quite some time after this ordeal. I had weeks of nightmares about the pain and begging the nurses not to hurt me.

So here I am now, a number of years later. For the most part, I have recovered physically and psychologically, but emotionally, I don't know if I ever will. Friends and family that are getting pregnant, having babies, and making memories surround me. I feel the sadness and the loss of knowing this isn't part of my journey, but when you can accept that your journey is yours alone, it becomes easier to surrender it and just love what *is*.

I am so grateful and thankful for my amazing life. I truly love what is. I have learned to love my journey and all its scars. Perhaps one day, they won't hurt so bad.

Vanessa Cañas

Vanessa is the founder of MasterMind4Kids, a global organization dedicated to teaching mindfulness and universal laws to orphan and inner-city children under the age of nine.

She is also an event consultant and empowers others to manage their own events.

Prior to entrepreneurship, Vanessa worked in corporate for seventeen years leading teams, large events, and implementing positive change leadership with United Airlines, GE Medical Systems, and AT&T.

Vanessa lives outside of Chicago with Jesse, her husband of twenty-four years, and their dog Olivia. They have one son, Nathan. Vanessa loves fast cars, music, and traveling with her husband.

Find Vanessa online:

http://www.vanessacanas.com/
https://www.linkedin.com/in/vanessa-cañas
http://bit.ly/VanessaCanas

Chapter 7

We All Have the Power

By Vanessa Cañas

A year-and-a-half has passed since I made the decision to start living a happier life. At the time, I had no idea how to start. However, I knew deep down that a change had to occur. I was in a great marriage and had a loving family. So why was I not satisfied? The work I was tasked with in corporate was not lighting me up like it did before. I no longer had any desire to work for someone else. I wanted to fly alone.

After deciding I wanted to make a change, I kept having an urge to read certain social media posts that I found enlightening. At the time, I was curious about entering the entrepreneurial world and leaving corporate for good.

Two months later, my Mom passed away. Three weeks after that, bam, I was laid off from corporate and had the opportunity to start my own business.

It's interesting how my impulse to learn was there right before the next step... and this is how it all started.

The million-dollar question: what was I going to teach or what service would I provide? At first, relationship coaching bubbled up simply because I have over twenty-five years under my belt with my best friend and husband. We are happy together, have a steamy relationship, and we've learned a tremendous amount over the years. Close family and friends tend to reach out to me when they are having difficulties, and my help seems to better their situation.

Right away, I started working on my visibility and sharing my expertise. Since I had no connections on social media, I made them locally in my community. I would wake up each day and decide what two or three steps I needed to take to get my name out in the world as a relationship expert. I started asking myself, *What can I do next Vanessa?*

Sometimes the hints would come and other times, nothing. I realized I wanted to hear the answers more often, so the search for more information was on to help me understand what I was missing. I began reading about our minds, our consciousness, and universal laws.

If you have the urge to read or learn about something, then act on it and do it. There's a reason, always.

Immediately after a few 'a-has' hit me over the head, two critical components were added to my life—meditation and journaling. These methods resonated the best with me. I discovered that writing my thoughts down felt like a release. I was no longer holding onto those thoughts, and I felt a little lighter each time. I also started writing about my dreams and what my future looked like. I would visualize it and write it down. In the beginning, I was very general about my dreams, but now I'm specific as I realized that there's tremendous power behind this.

Adding meditation was a whole new ball game for me. Before researching, I felt meditation was for the monks of the world, or for people who are happy and calm all the time. It never occurred to me that they were happy and calm *because* they meditated. I learned the goal of meditation is to quiet the conscious mind. By quieting the mind, new ideas find a way to flow in because the constant static has subsided. That made sense to me, so I ventured into meditating.

At first, I wondered if I was doing it right. I would sit quietly and try to focus on one thing, a calming sound like water, soothing music, or the birds singing outside. The problem was my brain seemed to be overly stimulated, and I could not focus at all. I would start thinking about the nonsense of the day, a problem I was trying to solve, or what to get at the market, or when to walk the dog. I mean my brain was *on*, and after a couple of days, I wondered what in the world I was doing wrong.

The good news is there is no right or wrong way to meditate. Everyone finds the right method for them. It takes patience. Patience with the goal to focus on one sound only and shutting down the mind as much as possible. After several days of trying to focus, I discovered that I was able to quiet my mind for a minute. It was always toward the end of my twenty minutes of meditating. Which meant I was unfocused for most of the time.

I decided I would take meditation slowly, be patient with myself, and practice it daily. I also found it soothing to take time during the day and appreciate what I had accomplished thus far. I called these gratitude moments. Taking the time to thank myself was, and is, powerful. I thank those that bring light into my life, and I'm thankful for the lessons I've learned. I took the time to do this daily because I felt healthy and happy. One of my goals is to be happier and practicing this daily clearly helped strengthen that goal.

After a couple of weeks of this, I started waking up with the idea that I should start managing events. I have over seventeen years of experience in corporate and as a consultant. I enjoy management, so I began thinking about offering this service instead of relationship coaching. However, I hesitated to act on it.

During this same time, I met someone online that was looking for help with an event in New York. It was a women's empowerment event, and I had been following some of the speakers since the earliest stages of my journey. I felt this was an opportunity to meet them. I didn't know much about the event host, but I knew a few of the speakers, so I focused on that.

The event was executed well in a short space of time, and I realized on day two that I needed to shift my focus to event management. I felt entrepreneurs would appreciate my style and business background, so I made the switch right away. For the next two months, my revenue hit over $10,000. I was in awe of the shift in income and the people coming my way.

I did notice some people I encountered were not quite on the same journey as myself. They were needy people, posing as aligned individuals, and somehow I felt I was the one to help them. At the time, I did not understand how damaging this was for my journey. I needed to focus on myself, get stronger, and then I could help others. I could not do it while getting there. The journey was meant for me alone.

I was blinded by my perspective of wanting to help others rather than focusing on building my event management business. In the process, I became unknowingly entangled with a con-artist that suffered from mental health issues. The woman was a pro at faking everything about herself. The only indicator I had (which I ignored) was my gut. From the first time I interacted with her, my gut instinct was uneasy. There was something about her that I could not pinpoint but I moved forward with her, thinking it was a sound relationship. It was not.

Trust your gut instinct above all else. If you have a spec of negative feelings toward someone, do not engage with them. If you must proceed, do so with caution.

After two great business months, the third turned out in the negative, several thousand dollars in the negative. It turns out the con-artist left me with the bill in hand for an event we planned. She took off. After finding out numerous facts about her and the family she came from, I realized this woman would never pay back the money she stole from others and me.

For me personally, this was devastating because I kept asking myself how I didn't see this coming? Why did this happen to me? I took a ride on a rollercoaster of negative emotions and was beating myself up pretty badly. I wasn't journaling, meditating or focusing on anything positive.

I contemplated going back to corporate for a hot second, but that just felt awful, so I knew I had to figure something out. All I wanted to do was stay in bed and cuddle with my dog Ollie. I didn't go out, stayed off social media, and joined the boo-hoo club. Well, that wasn't going to get me far very fast, I needed a swift kick in the behind to get going.

Then an angel walked into my life by the name of Reverend Danielle Randall. I had met Danielle before the shit hit the fan, but our contact was minimal. After this speed bump, Danielle and I spoke because she could see I was not in a good place. However, I was trying to come back out of it; I wasn't giving up!

She was the hand and the light that uplifted me. She reminded me that I am worthy of all that is good in life. I am not alone in this journey. God, the Universe, the Source, whatever you call them are always present and co-creating with me. I must know and trust this fact first before true alignment and clarity happens. We all have full access to this gift. It is up to us to re-align with the power we were born with. Do you ever wonder why children are so happy? They're aligned!

Take a moment and re-read the last paragraph. Pause and reflect on the power and insight this gives you as a human being. Understand and believe that we have a powerful guide within us at all times. The key is taking the time daily to stop, ask, and listen. That's where meditating plays a factor. Now I understood what needed to be done.

I had to take the bull by the horns and re-train my daily rituals and beliefs. I began to understand that I have the power to react and feel the way I want to feel. No one else has control.

Anyone that knew me back in the day would wonder how that was possible. I was a firecracker. It didn't take much to ignite me or get me involved in drama. I used to have road rage and a trucker mouth like no one else. Today, I am in full control of my reactions and how I wish to feel. I'm not 100% on the bandwagon, but I try, and it's a process that gets with every passing day. So how did I do this?

I decided to start journaling and meditating again. Making a decision and holding yourself to it is crucial. I blocked off my mornings for myself and shared my new plans with my husband. Taking care of myself was the priority. I also started to ask my inner being questions for guidance. I was reconnecting with the God within me because I had shut down communications years ago.

This is a sample conversation I have with myself in the morning or at night: "My God within, what is the best next step for me in my event management business? (I am specific with the request).

Show me the least difficult path; give me clarity. I am a child of God, and I deserve all the good in the world so I can spread more good. I ask for your guidance and thank you for being a part of my life-long journey. I am so happy I discovered you, and it feels so good. I never feel alone anymore, and that rocks! I am always in divine company. I am thankful for all my angels and guides that led me here. Thank you for helping me get closer and closer to my clarity. Every day is better than the day before, and I'm having fun! I know everything works out for me. Thank you! I love you!"

I share this with you because, at first, I had no idea how to ask. Again, there is no wrong way of asking, just ask from your heart. Don't focus on how to get the task done either. When something happens in business, our knee-jerk reaction is to act upon that situation; however, this may not always result in the best outcome because we are reacting from emotion or fear.

During this process, I was also facing bills piling up and possible foreclosure. I was having a difficult time practicing a positive mindset while my reality was front and center, flashing like a neon sign. *How do I overcome my scarcity mindset when my reality looks like this?* I thought to myself. Holy smokes, talk about a mental challenge. I realized that if I kept my worry and fear ignited all day, I would only get more of that. I had to turn it around and trust everything was going to work out. I had to feel what it was like on the other side where bills are not an issue, and money is flowing in steadily. I trusted, and each time something positive happened so we could pass the next hurdle.

This new way of guiding my feelings has worked out very well. When a situation arises, I feel uneasy, and thoughts flood into my mind. I stop myself immediately—before the negative feeling gets any momentum, and I tell myself, "Vanessa, what do you think about this? How do you feel about this?" I silence myself and breathe for as long as I have to until I can hear my heartbeat calming down and my only focus is how I want to feel. I want the solution to feel good. I want it to turn out well. I concentrate on those feelings to shift the energy.

Sometimes I even take a nap, especially when I can't focus at all. I have a million thoughts running in my head, so I put on soothing water sounds, and I take a nap. It works! It's like a reset button, and when I wake up, I chose to feel good and hopeful.

I will be honest and tell you this process is mentally challenging because most of us are wired slightly different because of our upbringing. I am a girl born in Chicago with immigrant parents and four siblings from El Salvador, Central America. I was taught that money didn't grow on trees and I had to work my ass off to make something of myself. Growing up eating rice and beans seeded mindset blocks around money and scarcity.

When it came to my feelings, I couldn't show any. I had to keep a serious face so that no one would mess with me. I was told that smiling or demonstrating happiness was a sign of weakness in a woman. I had to keep my tomboy appearance up at all times and hide my curves.

I realize my parents did the best they could, given the circumstances. They had limited information and had no idea they were skewing my mindset from a very early age. Even today, millions of parents are making negative statements in the household related to money, relationships, business, and politics, which directly affects how the children perceive these situations as adults. According to neurologists, all of our perceptions are seeded in our brain by the time we are nine-years-old. This awareness led to the birth of MasterMind4Kids. I'll elaborate on this later.

My point is that mindset work is a daily task. I am consciously aware of what I say, how I feel when I say it, and how I choose to react. In the past, all of this happened without my conscious awareness, so it's a whole new ball game in my head. I am aware now that I create my reality and I chose how I want to feel.

Be patient and loving with yourself while you're in the process; it takes time. I found this to be very comforting, and I'm nicer to myself because of it. I don't judge myself. It doesn't serve me.

How do I know that this process is working for me? There is no denying that the rendezvous with people that are aligned with my mission are making a positive impact on our world. The encounters I have are not by chance; they are directly aligned with something I am working on. I've found partners such as The Hawn Institute, and I've met people that are one degree of separation from the Obamas and Oprah. I've met Paula White and Marianne Williamson, and I've been invited by Arianna Huffington to join Thrive Global as a contributing writer. Clearly, these are indicators that I am on the right path, which means I continue to take daily action because this ride is a lot of fun!

We are meant to enjoy our lives and have fun. Working on our passions is a gift to ourselves. Everything flows with ease and grace. When speed bumps come along, we pivot, which typically leads to a better path.

How will you know if you're on track? You'll feel it. If you feel healthy and happy, you're on the right track. If you have any negative feelings coming through you, that means you're out of alignment, plain and simple. That's why it's a negative feeling; it's an indicator you need to recognize. Knowing what you don't want clears up your vision of what you do want. The contrast is there for us to choose which way to go.

Daily work on this is critical to your success and working your way closer to clarity; clarity that is undeniable to you and knowing what you have to do. You'll have no doubt. After months and months of conscious practice, I am happy to say that I am in a beautiful space of clarity and I know what my mission is in life. I'm getting steadier and steadier by the day.

I am now in a place where I ask, and answers come daily. I take those inspired actions and complete them. I have a sense of accomplishment daily because I know each step is closer to the next goal.

My ultimate goal is to launch MasterMind4Kids! This project is focused on orphan and inner-city children under the age of nine. The plan is to teach children about their minds and meditation. Mentoring them as they grow up and demonstrate a new way of living in which they are happy and confident enough to follow their dreams. We provide the tools for social success and awareness of universal laws while nurturing them into adulthood. I believe this effort is the start of a new generation of children who'll grow up with a positive outlook on themselves and life in general. It's empowering them to use their inner power to be, do, or have anything they want in life! Just like you can!

We all have access to this knowledge and truth. It is up to us to decide, act on it, allow it to come your way, and receive it. Once you commit, you will start to see life differently, and you'll be happier because of it.

I dare you to try focusing on yourself for forty-five days. Truly commit, learn more, practice what resonates the best with you, and watch what happens. You'll never go back to your old negative beliefs; you'll build new ones that serve you well.

You will feel your power within, and you'll love it! Trust me. I love you!

Kristi Candelario

As a little girl, Kristi wanted to become a fairy godmother, and as a business coach, she feels like she's living her childhood dream! She is devoted to empowering and teaching her clients to wonder less and wander more through their dream life with her structure, system, management, strategy, and streamline activities in place to promote the success they have craved for years.

Kristi has a degree in business management with the concentration of entrepreneurial studies. She has been a guest speaker/expert teacher on multiple business topics and has judged numerous business plan competitions. Kristi has helped many business owners create success, whether they are experienced or just starting out. Online business models, brick and mortar business models, and product launches; she has experienced it all.

She's all about taking her clients from the wishing phase and transforming their dreams into a real business with profits margins and freedom.

Find Kristi online:

http://kristicandelario.com

Chapter 8

Gambling Against the Odds

By Kristi Candelario

"Turn it around and hold it up to the light." My father held up my second-grade spelling test that was given to him by my teacher. At that moment, (not fully understanding what was being presented) he felt proud, and at the same time he gained clarity. The document was a mirrored image of the letters spelled correctly. Meaning I got a perfect score, but every word was spelled in reverse. I was diagnosed with a learning disability that year.

From then on, I was pulled from my class for half of the school day to attend special education to focus on my speech, reading, and writing. After second-grade, I attended summer school to catch up to my peers. All I wanted was to be 'normal.' I did my best to try to keep this part of my life private; the thought of being different was something I feared. My mother fought to keep me in as many 'normal' classes as she could. She knew I was consciously embarrassed and tried to keep what was left of my routine. She spent an abundance of time working with me one on one, and for that, I am forever grateful.

I began hating my 'norm' in school. I hated having attention drawn to me as I left the room to attend my special classes. I hated being called on in front of my peers because I was so scared I would not answer the question correctly, read properly, or pronounce the words right. Even worse, I had a fear that I would stutter while speaking. Any test that had a peer grading my exam scared the shit out of me because it would validate my vulnerability. I even hated when my brother and sister would ask me any questions. I didn't know how to help them, which made me feel less like their big sister. My response was always, "Go ask Mom." Most of all, I hated when someone would tease me. "Kristi spell, read, or say this word." If I could not answer correctly, I felt venerable, like a joke.

Often, we see others succeed and think that it happened effortlessly overnight. The truth is, it was not easy to transform my learning disability and it sure as hell wasn't easy to show up consistently. It took a lot of practice, patience, dedication, self-awareness, faith, time and tenacity. Even though this was an ongoing progression, there were still times I had the same fears as my second-grade self trapped inside me.

I graduated from the special education program at the end of my fourth-grade year. At the beginning of fifth-grade, I started my involvement in the dyslexia program. At the time, I was still being pulled from my classes, but only for an hour. By the time I started high school, I was no longer being pulled out of classes. Instead, I just had '504 Modifications.' I ended up graduating high school in the top 20% of my class with some college credits in my pocket. I then graduated college with my BBA in Business Management with the concentration of entrepreneurial studies in under four years, with no registered learning disabilities.

Embarrassing as it may sound, tenacity is a word I probably could not spell until high school. Nor did I know it's meaning, but tenacity is the first word that comes to mind when I think of my life. I have always been a dreamer and wishful thinker. To me, this word holds so much truth and value. I have felt like I was going to live an extraordinary life since I could remember. However, I also knew that I would have to be a tenacious fighter in order to go further on the journey I craved to travel during my lifetime.

While we are alive, we fear something each day, not knowing if it's our last day. I say this because you are alive at this moment and you have a chance to be tenacious and gamble against the odds to win. Many people live their life full of stress, fear, and regret, which essentially leaves them unfulfilled. I am a firm believer of dreams and living a life of pure freedom.

I had to work twice as hard to keep up with my peers in school. It was challenging at times, but I knew I could not give up. When it came to entrepreneurship, tenacity came into play once again. I was not the entrepreneur that created success overnight or even the one that created success in under a year-and-a-half in business.

The odds of winning the lottery are approximately one in fourteen million. A person has a one in three million chance of sighting a UFO. That's almost five times more likely than winning the jackpot. There is a one in nine million chance that you will be struck by lightning twice in your lifetime. When we gamble, the odds are usually 1%. Therefore, if there are over seven billion people on our planet and over one-and-a-half billion gamble per year, that means we have four-hundred-and fifty-nine people that overcome the odds in a single year. I was, and am, a fighter because I knew I would have to face unique battles that would be thrown at my dreams. I knew from my childhood that I would be a tenacious gambler at life. I had to be.

Entrepreneurial life has taught me that I don't want to be 'normal.' Being 'normal' meant I would be out of business within three years and stuck forever as a dreamer.

When I started my business on April Fools' Day 2015, I was not on the road to success. Everything felt like a shit storm that was happening painfully slowly. Failure came after each attempt I made. I ended up taking a six-month break from my dream business to re-evaluate myself, my dreams, my future, and my business. Not because I was busy, but because I did not want to be vulnerable and in my truth. However, as soon as I found my truth and my voice, the rest was history. I remember that day as if it was yesterday.

My husband and I were on our honeymoon in early June 2016 when ironically, I received the clarity I had been searching for since 2012 when I started dabbling into entrepreneurship. It was that moment I knew I had to get vulnerable and share all my unique experiences with the world. It was that moment that I made a promise to my husband that if I did not create success by our one-year anniversary, I would be signing divorce papers, or quitting my dream business for good. I risked the future and all my desires in the moment that I shifted into myself.

Naturally, the tenacious gambler in me came back, and I knew I had what it would take to make this work. I was no longer wondering and overthinking things; I was taking action without analyzing the outcome. It was that mindset and gamble that brought me to successfully launching a $20,000 program in less than six months.

If each of us is one in a million, then that means there are over seven thousand people just like you. The next time you wonder if you are capable of overcoming obstacles and beating the odds, remember there is someone just like *you* who has already achieved what you desire.

Trust in yourself and your desires more than anyone else in the world. That's the power you hold. You are the only authority you need. It really doesn't matter where you've been or where you're going; you can get there because you are human, just like me and everyone else you know. Don't be ashamed or scared; open your arms, heart, and ears so you can be ready to receive whatever your soul is seeking. You got this!

Lily Corinne

Lily Corinne is a mindset lifestyle coach, licensed massage therapist and reiki healer. She has ten years of experience in alternative health care. Her life's passion and purpose are to inspire, educate, and empower women. She does so with the knowledge that everything that one needs or wants is within them, they just have to tap into it.

She promotes alternative mindset and lifestyle shifts so women can take back their power and happiness in order to prevent stress overload, anxiety and burnout. She is the mother of three wonderful young adults who are her pride and joy.

Find Lily online:

https://www.facebook.com/ChoosetobeAWESOME/
https://www.facebook.com/groups/559451317547374/

Chapter 9

The Journey to Within

By Lily Corinne

In the spring of 2001, I was twenty-three-years-old, raising three young children while working, and going to college. It was a lot, but I was young so, the world was my oyster, right? At least that's what I always thought. One day that spring, the kids and I were visiting at my parents' house. I was sitting in the recliner watching Oprah when all of the sudden I felt a rush of warmth come over me like a blanket.

I started to feel my stomach turning upside down, and then it dropped to my toes, while at the same time my heart began to beat so hard that it felt as if it was about to pound out of my chest. Every hair on my body stood straight. I was hot and cold all at the same time. It felt as though all of my bodily functions were going to give out. Adrenaline frantically rushed through my veins like a faucet that was turned on full power. My chest became tighter and tighter with every second, and breathing was such an intense struggle. Then my head started spinning, as if I was falling into a tunnel, down a vicious spiral into nowhere. The floor was blurred and wavy like water; the ceiling seemed to be floating away. It was almost as if I was in a house of mirrors; everything was distorted.

Several thoughts ran through my mind. *What is happening to me? Am I losing my mind? Am I having a nervous breakdown?* Unbalanced and shaking I walked over to my sister, who we just picked up from college in Ohio. Tears were running down my face. I said to her, "Please tell the kids that I love them so much and that they are the world to me and I'm so sorry this happened." I was bawling my eyes out excessively, my knees gave out, and I fell to the floor. I just wanted to curl up in a ball in the fetal position. I started rocking back and forth; I couldn't stop shaking. I wanted somebody to give me a shot of tranquilizer to knock me out and make it all better.

My mom arrived and helped my sister walk me to the bedroom so I could lie down on the bed. As I lay there, my mom covered me up. I could tell they were shocked and scared for me. I shook vigorously, wondering what was going on. My mom rested her arms on my legs, trying to comfort me and held my legs down as they were shaking too much. I remember her reassuring me that everything was ok as tears slipped down her cheeks.

I did not want her to stop holding my legs because the comfort of it just made me feel a little bit more grounded (I didn't even know that was the right term at the time). In hindsight the warmth and comfort made me feel like what I was experiencing was real. That was my only grasp of sanity and serenity!

I don't remember anything else from that day after that. I could probably guess that I finally collapsed due to exhaustion and slept for fifteen hours straight. I now know that I had a full-blown panic attack. This was caused by stress and anxiety that had built up until my body until I hit a breaking point. It was one of the scariest things I have ever experienced.

Many traumatic things had happened in my life leading up to this, and any one of them alone probably could have set off this panic attack—but why was this the breaking point? What was different this time? Why was this my limit? Was my body trying to tell me something? Maybe the Universe wanted to tell me something?

In hindsight, it makes a lot of sense. I was a young mother, only twenty-three with three kids under the age of eight. I was also a newly single mom because I finally ended the abusive relationship I was in for six years. I was in my third year of college, ready to graduate in a year with a marketing degree, while at the same time working thirty hours a week at a department store. I was struggling financially to make ends meet. I was fortunate enough to have financial and babysitting help from my parents, but the stress was still there.

I would like to say that I was an honorable, strong woman who knew what she needed to do and who she needed to be, and prevailed with flying colors. However, that just isn't the truth. Much of the time, I was on autopilot and did what I had to do because it needed to be done (even if I wasn't doing it right). Therein lies the problem; I wasn't 'mindfully' living. I believe that so many moms (and people in general) operate this way... sadly. We are needed to be everything for everyone—all of the time. We have to start giving ourselves a break and begin to take time for self-care and gentle understanding. This equals mindful living. Having said that, looking back what did I expect would happen when I was living on burnout mode with no self-care!?

This breakdown was truly a blessing in disguise. I was forced to face my fears, and release them. Subsequently, I released my past deep traumas, found my inner-strength—not just the strength that I had been using up until then—but also the unwavering, limitless strength that I was unaware of. Then I learned how to tap into that divine power.

This strength was always there, deep within my soul center. This power is within the energetic field of limitlessness that we all are a part of. The power that comes with this kind of force is the creative and healing power of the source, God, the Universe.

I learned little by little, and it started me on a journey to an enormous thirst for knowledge of what this all meant, and what was possible in life. I sought out every little piece of information I could find. I followed my intuition, which led me to the first piece of knowledge I acquired: the key to living a fulfilled and happy life.

Soon after, I enrolled in school to become a massage therapist. While in massage school, I had an intuition to get involved in energy healing and explore all of the facets of it. Month after month, I continued to learn priceless teachings and tools.

There are so many unique and fun ways to deal with stress in our lives. We don't have to come to a breaking point (a nervous breakdown or panic attack) before we wake up and deal with it. Dealing with it, to me, used to mean taking anxiety and depression medications while attending therapy sessions. I certainly don't discount medicine or therapy. They can, and do serve a purpose. Having a therapist, coach or accountability partner and taking needed medication has been important for me. However, in conjunction, the inner work that needs to be done has been integral.

There is a serenity knowing that there are limitless options available to me to have serenity, and for me to create the life I want. This mindset shift started with me implementing and practicing alternative modalities such as visualization and meditation, in moments where my anxiety and stress came up. As I would feel them work, I started to believe that we have all we need inside of us and we always have the option to feel safe and secure. These tools have always been there. We've just forgotten how to use them.

Becoming more mindful on a daily basis is a great beginning. The idea is to live mindfully in each present moment while appreciating each breath. This however, is the complete opposite of what we are taught in Western society—we usually brag about how little sleep we are running on. This is not physically, emotionally or mentally healthy. It's my belief that we need to look more to the practices of Eastern society in regards to managing stress and maintaining overall health.

It is so important that we take the time for self-care to prevent and reduce stress, and therefore prevent anxiety and depression. It shouldn't have to come to the point of having a panic attack or a nervous breakdown for you to start taking care of your stress levels and overall emotional health.

We can start taking care of ourselves now, the smart way and truly live how we aspire to live before the chaos of life gets in the way. The whole process of going on this quest for knowledge and enlightenment has been such an immense spiritual journey for me—body, mind, and soul.

The discovery of this incredible strength and power has given me the motivation and inspiration to fulfill my life purpose and passion. One of the ways I do this is by educating woman with the knowledge that we all have this limitless soul-centered strength and power within us available at any time.

We need to fill our toolbox with meditation, visualization, reiki healing, massage, EFT tapping, affirmations, whole foods, exercise and so many other different modalities and practices to live mindful and connected lives.

While navigating through this ever evolving rollercoaster called life, to hold serenity, comfort, and certainty, one needs to feel a strong sense of knowing that there is something or someone (the source, God, or the Universe) looking over them, protecting them and guiding them to all that is good. Without that sense of safety, security, belief and knowing the world can seem like a very scary and lonely place. That scared and lonely place is where stress, anxiety, depression and burnout live.

I—like most people—have always wanted to live a happy, healthy, fulfilling, and exciting life. So just the knowing that we, ourselves have the power to do, be or have anything we want in life, and that there is nothing to fear was a huge epiphany for me! There was so much I didn't know we had the ability to access and tap into as human beings. An entirely new world, the metaphysical world, the infinite power, and energy of the Universe. The realization that this knowledge could not only be utilized for myself, but also for my children, family, and friends was so exciting.

When you take the time to tap in and feel the infinite power, strength, connection and expansion of the Universe, the unlimited possibilities, your life will be changed forever.

I intend to live my life honoring myself while being kind, loving, and always following my intuition. I intend to be the very best mama that I can be to my three precious children. My mission is to educate women about alternative self-care, mindset and lifestyle shifts so they can take back their power and step into their happiness.

Jennifer Flores

Jennifer is a single mother to two vivacious teenagers. She has a background in marriage and family therapy focusing on individuals, couples, and women who have experienced sexual betrayal by a romantic partner. Jennifer has extensive experience in sex addiction recovery, betrayal trauma and is pre-certified through Dr. Doug Weiss.

She is currently a transformational strategist coach working with individuals one on one as well as in a group setting to create the best life possible. She also coaches women to move beyond betrayal.

Jennifer's best work is helping individuals find purpose as well as guiding individuals who are 'stuck,' to move forward. She is described as intuitive and solution focused.

Find Jennifer online:

https://www.facebook.com/intentionallivingwithjenn/
metamorphosiswithjenn@gmail.com

Chapter 10

Finding Me Again

By Jennifer Flores

"I give up, and I give in." Those were the words that changed the course of my life. I remember it like it was yesterday. I sat on the edge of my bed just hours after another failed relationship. I wasn't even thirty, and I had two failed marriages. I suppose if I was a movie star it would be more acceptable, but I wasn't—I was the producer, director, and actor in my personal low budget film that didn't quite make it.

It was close to midnight, and the fight I had to keep running from had taken its toll. It wasn't the failed relationships that had me curled up in a ball on the hardwood floor; it was a 'failed life,' 'failed dreams,' 'failed career,' and the list of other 'failures' that flooded my mind as I lay in a puddle of tears. I had no one to blame and nowhere to turn but inward. I knew it was time; time to set this circus down, get real with myself and figure out this thing called life.

When I was a little girl, I used to stare out my window, and when I'd hear an airplane fly by my heart felt sad and excited all at the same time. I thought if could just get on that plane, I could go anywhere, anywhere but here. I could finally explore and escape the pain I was feeling daily from living in a dysfunctional home environment.

At the age of seven, I knew I wanted to become a lawyer. Don't ask me how I came to that conclusion; perhaps it was from a show I watched. Nevertheless, the thought of wearing high heels and a perfectly crisp suit, walking into a courtroom to argue my point just felt right. I knew there was a great big world out there and I wanted to be part of it. I dreamed of the day I'd marry and move out or the day I would 'make it big' when I became a lawyer. I dreamed as I stared out the window. However, deep down, I felt stuck.

Shortly after my preteen years I began my journey of 'exploring and escaping' my reality in an unhealthy way. I started acting out and running away when I was about thirteen-years-old. I was raised in a strict conservative home where rules proceeded relationships, where love came with a price. It was dysfunctional in every way possible.

Somewhere inside I knew there was more to life, but I didn't quite know what that meant. One day (during time I was running away frequently), I came home and had not noticed that I had missed my menstrual cycle. My mother took me to the doctor, and I can still remember her coming out of the exam room saying "Congratulations Grandma."

I was pregnant. I was fifteen-years-old and pregnant. I knew I needed to change and I desired to be a good mom. Many people told my mother that I should give my baby up for adoption, but I knew that wasn't what I wanted. Nine months later, I gave birth to the most beautiful brown-eyed girl with deep dimples. She was beyond perfect. All six pounds of her were perfect.

I was doing adult things, but I didn't *really* know what love was. Chaos was very familiar to me; it almost felt like 'home.' My daughter's father was no exception to the continued chaos. I decided it was best to raise my baby on my own with the help of my family.

I went back to high school, met someone, got pregnant again, was married by seventeen, had baby number two at eighteen and was divorced by nineteen.

Something changed in me when I entered junior college. No one knew my past, or me and it was a place to compensate for all the 'mistakes' I made up until then.

Compensation was not a word, but a lifestyle I cultivated. I began layering myself with a shallow version of who I thought I wanted to be, and with each layer it kept people out, protected my shame, and kept me from fully showing up to life. I went from one unhealthy relationship to the next. I lived in the fast lane, and on the outside, all looked well. I traveled, had friends, I was doing well in college, and my children were healthy. However, all the while, I was dying inside, yet, I couldn't understand why. I kept searching for meaning, and every decision I made was a means to an end. I became good at mimicking others, believing, if I acted a certain way I'd 'find' myself. As time went on, I met someone and thought it was a good idea to marry again because I was older. I didn't know the pain that lay ahead. Nor did I know that this pain was for my own good.

I remember talking to a friend just a few years before I remarried. Her husband had cheated on her numerous times. I thought to myself; *I'd never stay with a cheater.* I told her on many occasions that she should leave. In all honesty, I assumed she was weak, ignorant, and desperate. I can remember the day I discovered that gnawing feeling in the pit of my stomach was intuition telling me something was off in my relationship. So I did what I knew best. I lost weight, put on a pretty dress, cleaned more, did my makeup more, tried to be nicer. The list of 'mores' went on.

The night I discovered the pornography, the online chat rooms, multiple texts, and nude photos of women on his phone I felt a pain I had never experienced before. It felt like someone punched me in the gut. I sat there paralyzed. The rage I felt frightened me. I confronted him but was met with denial and blame. I just wasn't enough, and I couldn't understand why. I guess God has a way of humbling you, as I did the exact opposite of what I told my friend years before when her partner cheated! I finally understood why she stayed. She wasn't weak at all; in fact, she bravely fought for her dream and her family. I tried to do the same. I did more and yet a part of my soul had died as I compromised more and more of myself every day. I did things and said things I was ashamed of. In the end, we didn't make it. I'll never look at women who stays with her partner in the same judgmental way. There is no shame in wanting to see redemption take place.

Years later, I thought I'd put this story behind me when I met someone else. We dated for a period, and yet again, I found myself betrayed by a man. I didn't stay as long as I did with my ex. However, I stayed long enough to lose more parts of myself. I didn't know a human soul could hurt so much. I didn't know shame could cripple one's heart.

During that time, I successfully finished my masters, and I thought this was it; life would finally turn a new leaf. Instead, it took an unexpected turn. I fell into a deep depression. The shame of experiencing depression was torture. The energy I expended trying to hide my feelings from others took its toll. At one point, I was so suicidal that I had a plan, a very *detailed* plan. I felt my children deserved a better mother and I had lost all faith in my ability to lead a healthy whole life. I no longer trusted myself. I hated myself. Deep inside I was desperate for change. Desperate to start over again. Desperate to be free. Desperate to dream again.

Lying on the floor that night, I hit rock bottom. I could hardly summon the energy to get up. I didn't want to move. I thought if I just lay there long enough God would show up, because I had run out of bright ideas. I had no fight left in me. When I finally got up, God showed up in a way I never expected. There was no white dove at my window and no overwhelming sense of peace, but, a new fight. A fight to live. I decided I wanted a do-over. I wanted to discover who I was meant to be not who I thought I needed to be. I didn't know how or where to begin, but I was willing to lean into life, lean into pain, and lean into hard places.

I woke up with renewed hope. Rock bottom was the place in which I rebuilt my life from the inside out. I don't think I cried so much in my life as I did during that dark season. I planned time to be alone to journal, pray, and cry. I finally got real with God, and myself. I wasn't willing to hide anymore. I went to therapy, attended a support group and for the first time in my life I spoke about my experience with shame. All of it: the abuse from childhood, acting out as a teenager, betrayal, career failure, and my struggle with depression.

Something sacred takes place when shame is exposed. It has to die, and indeed, it did. Not in one sitting. It was one big yes followed by, thousands if not more, smaller yeses. I said yes to showing up to life even if it didn't make sense. I said yes to processing more shame, I said yes to living authentically, I said yes to deciding life was good even with all the 'bad' parts, and most importantly I said yes to living with more intention. I intentionally looked for all the good in my life, including my past. I have the utmost compassion for my younger self. I see her, not as a distant part of me, but a golden link to my good, to where I was always meant to be…it just took me a little longer than most.

When I look at pictures of myself from many years ago, I can see the girl who was once lost and the parts of me who had the best intentions, but who just didn't quite understand the true meaning of life. I'm grateful for those dark days because rainbows show up after a storm. No, life is not *always* rainbows and unicorns. In fact, life can still be hard, especially now that I'm raising two teenagers who constantly teach me about going with the flow of life.

Most nights when I get home from work, I look forward to a good movie or TV show. You know the ones where there's a happy ending, and there's usually a hero to save the day. My story certainly didn't have that fairy tale ending with someone rescuing me. It is still evolving, and the best part is I was my *own* hero. I showed up to save the day in the nick of time. I found purpose.

Purpose is simple; it's creating more experience that leads to new awareness. It expands my abilities, and I know I can do more than I ever thought possible. One of my purposes has been working as a transformational coach. I work with individuals one on one and in groups to find purpose and transform their lives, mindset, narrative, and business.

Family and friends told me many times that God would not waste my pain. At the time, in all honesty, it infuriated me, but that statement and promise have been so true in my life. I also coach women who have felt the pain of betrayal to find purpose and dream again. I help those whose partners choose to walk out or who are ready to reclaim their life and live well after the 'storm.' My heart is so full when I walk beside an individual who is ready for life change.

I wake up each morning, and it's hard not to be truly grateful for all that life has to offer. I used to believe I was damaged goods, destined for failure, but all that changed the night I said, "I give up and I give in." I gave up running and settling. I gave up pretending, and I started living with intention and purpose. I found a new meaning to life that is not limited to external things. I found I have all I need inside of me. Sure, there are areas that still need tending to, and that's ok because I never want to stop learning or growing and I never want to stop living. Living for years in a body I hated, in a world that was dark, and experiencing limited beliefs that held me captive is a space I no longer am willing to go back to. I had to go to some dark and hard places to find myself. I'm a believer that if we lean into life, miracles happen. I'm forever grateful for second chances and to truly dream again.

There are no prerequisites for worthiness.

~Brené Brown

Daniel Fung

Daniel Fung is a solopreneur, business, life, accountability and text coach. More importantly, he is known as the DreamMaker.

Daniel is living his dream and wants to inspire, empower, and transform millions of individuals to do the same. By applying the tools and techniques that he's learned, he has been able to accomplish many things that once seemed impossible. Daniel is an inspiration to many of his clients and has helped transform some with just one coaching session.

Daniel is an INFP, and his gallup strength is learner; achiever; futuristic; ideation and activator.

Book a thirty-minute clarity call with him and prepare yourself for an incredible journey.

Find Daniel online:

www.whatareyouafearof.com
www.askdanielfung.com
www.danielfung.com

Chapter 11

Father Doesn't Know Best

By Daniel Fung

My father stood over me; wide-eyed in anger. "You're going to the University of British Columbia because all your cousins went there," he roared.

My heart sank as his words shattered my dreams. My goal was to enroll in the electronics technology program at the British Columbia Institute of Technology after my high school graduation, and then spend my life designing next generation technology.

I've never felt in control of my destiny. I was born into a typical Asian household. I'm sure you've heard it before; go to school, earn excellent grades; get a good job, (doctor, accountant, or engineer); get married to an Asian; have kids and be happy for the rest of your life. It sounds like a fairy tale doesn't it? The only problem was that it wasn't *my dream*. It was my parents' dream, and they wanted me to live my life the way *they* wanted.

My father worked as an auto body repairman, and I was in awe of his talents. I remembered many people calling him to work on side jobs. My mom was a seamstress and brought piecework home to make a few extra bucks. My grandmother would look after my sister and me during the day. This too was typical of an Asian family. I realize now that my parents worked incredibly hard to provide a better life for us. They were also sponsoring my uncles from China to Canada, so they too could have a better life.

Status is paramount in the Asian community; financial wealth, what university your kids attended, what kind of cars you drove, the number of grandkids you had, etc. Bragging rights are everything. I remember my mom playing mahjong with her friends. Their conversation consisted of them trying to convince each other that *their* kids were the best. I felt like a pawn on a chessboard.

My earliest memory is of my mother teaching me how to count when I was three. This wasn't your regular counting from one to ten. That wouldn't have been challenging enough. Her children counted to one-hundred. I still remember saying "ninety-eight, ninety-nine." I would pause, smile, and then yell, "One-hundred." The sense of accomplishment and joy was incredible. I still feel proud as I write about it here.

With my grandmother looking after us during the day, I had a lot of spare time. I was very curious and loved tinkering and experimenting. My fondest experimenting memory involves the television and radio. I believed that if I placed the radio behind the television and tuned it to a channel that was displaying snow (black and white dots) I would be able to see the person from the radio appear on the television.

I also dismantled radios and televisions and tried putting them back together, unsuccessfully of course. I would then get into trouble. Whenever my sister or I got into trouble, we would have to stand with our heads facing the corner while holding our ear lobes, and remain silent. This could last anywhere from fifteen minutes to a couple of hours. It was my parents' form of punishment.

Fast forward to grade six and my environment was very different. I was expected to have large amounts of homework every day, and if I didn't bring home enough, my aunt would assign extra, or my mom would order me to write my Chinese name one-hundred times (馮朝敬). I decided to take matters into my own hands. When I didn't have any homework, I would deliberately go ahead of the lesson plan. This worked well for me. My teacher never held me back; she encouraged my thirst for knowledge, and I loved it. More about her later on.

In high school, it was pretty much the same. My curiosity helped me excel. My favorite subjects were math, electronics, and physics. I remembered getting a very high score in one of my physics tests, and the teacher held up the paper and showed everyone in class. I was embarrassed. He said that physics didn't have to be hard as long as you understood it. He spoke about how little I wrote on the test, and yet it was exactly what he was looking for. I remembered him saying, "Keep it short and simple." That phrase became my mantra.

I also did very well in my electronics' courses. I had an excellent understanding of the subject. I designed and built many projects. I knew this was the path I wanted to take, but as you've seen from the start of my story, my father had other ideas. I had no choice but to attend the University of British Columbia because he was paying for my tuition.

Due to my upbringing, I did very well in my science and math. In math, I received a final grade of 105% (with bonus marks). In my second year of university, I worked and saved enough to pay for the following year's tuition. I was accepted into an engineering program. That's when everything went downhill. It seemed as though someone had blown out my candle. I noticed that my understanding of the subjects was sub-par, and I didn't know why.

There was a tutorial session, and the teaching assistant was ill, so the professor took his place. He spent an hour going over one question and at the end of the session, he said, "Oops, sorry guys, I did it wrong." I was furious. I paid good money to go to school, and I got a professor who didn't know his stuff. What a joke.

The next day, I went to the Dean of Engineering and told him what transpired. He consoled me and said that all the distinguished professors left for universities that paid more. He asked if I wanted to leave the program and get my full tuition back. I said, yes immediately.

Now, I had a bigger problem. What was I to tell my father? It took me two weeks to gather enough courage and tell him that I dropped out of university. He was angry, but his main concern was how he was going to explain this to his brothers. I felt awful, like his brothers' opinions meant more than mine did.

A couple of weeks later something miraculous occurred. My father pulled me aside and said, "It's your life, I want you to be happy." He left me alone. I was motionless for a few minutes and I didn't know how to react. For the first time in my life I was free to follow my destiny. I felt such joy at the prospect of choosing my own path. This led me to enroll at BCIT and attend their electronics technology program.

At BCIT, I had no social life, which was all right with me as I'm an introvert. I worked hard and received high marks on every subject. It was here that I appreciated my strict upbringing. I was able to achieve maximum results with minimal study. While my friends were stressing out, I felt confident in my abilities. People looked up to me, and I didn't mind helping them.

I graduated from the electronics technology program with honors and received a scholarship.

A hi-tech company hired me, and within a few months, I had my dream job designing and building products, which went well for about two years. During this time, the company's sales skyrocketed, and our parent company could no longer do our purchasing. The vice-president pointed at me and said that I was now the purchaser. He stated that I knew most of the vendors and that I would be good at it. I didn't have the courage to decline my new role, as I was afraid that I would be fired. I took on the new position with little knowledge of what was expected of me. I learned quickly and became an SCMP (supply chain management professional). I was now a professional purchaser, and no longer had my dream job.

As a purchaser, I met many people who were willing to help out. I remember one acquaintance that said, "It's not what you know, it's who you know, and it's who *they* know that will help you get things done faster. All you have to do is ask." Being young, I disregarded his words. You go to school, get educated and start from ground zero to make a name for yourself. He didn't argue with me and just told me to remember what he had said. That was almost thirty years ago. As I get older and wiser, this phrase rings a lot of truth.

I started dating when I joined the hi-tech firm. I was quite shy, so my friends introduced me to a girl they had known for quite some time. We dated a few times, and then my father found out.

"You better break up with that white girl, or you'll have to move out," he screamed. I felt so defeated. This just *didn't happen* in an Asian family. You're supposed to live with your parents until you get married. This outburst from my father was his way of telling me that if I didn't break up with my girlfriend, he was going to disown me. I couldn't think of anything worse.

Interestingly enough, two weeks later, he approached me and said, "It's your life, I want you to be happy." I realized later on that he worked for someone that knew my girlfriend's sister. He had told my father to look at life differently. He reminded him that he was in Canada and shouldn't stick so rigidly to the old customs. Canada is a melting pot of cultures and that's what makes it a great place to live.

My girlfriend soon became my wife. When she gave birth to our first child, my father held my daughter for over two hours. I remember my wife getting jealous because he was holding onto our daughter longer than she did. I told her it was a good thing. We now have four children, three boys, and one girl. My father is happy.

My home life was perfect, but I was not satisfied at work. Something was missing, but I didn't know what. I decided to leave my job after eight years. I worked at six other companies before discovering what was missing. I had the tools to become whatever I wanted. My parents made sure of that, but I wanted a job that I loved.

At my last place of employment, there was a calling, and through unrelated events, I found myself looking at Rhonda Britten's website (www.rhondabritten.com). I spent half an hour reading it. I realized that I wanted to become a life coach and I enrolled right away.

In November 2014, I told my coach that I had wanted to transition from my current job to a full-time life coach in five years. That was cut short—*very* short.

In April 2015, my manager and the HR VP came into my office. I knew what was going on right away. They were going to let me go. I felt uneasy for a moment, as if my world had ended, but I shook my manager's hand and thanked him for helping me to make a decision that I couldn't make. He set me free from twenty-five years of mediocrity.

I took a blank piece of paper and said to him, "You see this blank piece of paper? I can now do whatever I want, with whomever I want, whenever I want, wherever I want."

"I don't get it." he replied.

"You don't have to get it; I got it," I responded.

I gathered my belongings and left corporate life for good. My dream of becoming a full-time life coach became a reality in just five months; I didn't have to wait five years.

This was the beginning of the rest of my life. I don't call it work, it's more like play. Transforming the lives of others brings me such joy. My goal is to inspire a million lives. I want to give them a sense of hope that anything is possible. If you set your intentions correctly and take action, you will achieve your dreams. I don't call myself a coach because many people have a tough time understanding what a coach does. I call myself the DreamMaker and they understand that. It's short and simple.

Someone once asked me who had been the most influential teacher during my school years. Without a doubt, it was my grade six/seven teacher, Mrs. Fester who I hadn't seen for forty years. I've always said that I'd love to meet her again, and in October

2016 somehow the stars lined up. From a series of unrelated events, I checked my cousin's Facebook page, and there was a mention of Mrs. Fester's 80th birthday party. I scrolled down the comments and saw a familiar name, so I took the chance of sending her a message. A few weeks later, she met me with open arms. We hugged for quite some time, and I was so elated. I spent five hours talking to her. I wanted to make sure she knew what a positive influence she had on my life. I owe her a lot.

In November 2016, I told a friend that I would realize my dream of writing a book, and here I am. Within a short few years, I've achieved things I never thought possible. I attribute this to learning how to step out of my comfort zone. I've gained so much confidence and courage. I am *comfortable* with being *uncomfortable*.

I now enjoy life, the way it's meant to be enjoyed. I often think of my father's words, and how they set me on a determined path to a future *I wanted*. His love was tough, but it allowed me to see how important it is to follow your dreams. In turn, this has allowed me to help others find *their* path so they can become who they are meant to be.

I'm living *my* dreams....so can you. Don't let other people influence you to live *their* dreams.

Candace Gish

Located in Westerose, Alberta, host, and founder of Divas That Care, Candace Gish knows what its like to be an entrepreneur, have an idea and build a solid business.

When she's not talking with the Divas on her radio show, building her network marketing business, homeschooling her four daughters or volunteering, you will find her curled up with a great book, doing traditional rug hooking, gardening or traveling.

Find Candace online:

www.divasthatcare.com
twitter.com/@divasthatcare
www.facebook.com/divasthatcare

Chapter 12

Diva in the Making

By Candace Gish

Looking back, it amazes me on how it all began.

I remember August 2008 as if it was yesterday. My husband and I decided it was time for me to quit my job as a financial planner so I could stay at home with our growing family. We made the decision to homeschool our oldest daughter because she was behind academically and we wanted to help her catch up. Homeschooling was very stressful that year because we didn't know what we were doing and few people supported us. Little did I know it was the best decision ever we ever made, as it helped steer our journey to financial freedom.

That was the beginning of a very busy time in our lives. A time that brought much personal heartache and growth. That fall I found out that we were also expecting a new baby. That is a lot of change in a short period, and I started to worry about contributing financially. Having that background as a financial planner and having owned businesses before being married, I felt constricted in many ways. I had been an independent woman for so many years, and it felt strange not having my own income. This may sound strange but I enjoyed making my own money, and I didn't feel guilty when I spent it.

My husband was a very hard worker and spent many hours away from home to make sure that we were ok. This caused much personal guilt on my part, and I wanted to find a way to alleviate some of the stress he was feeling. I know he wanted to be around more, but he didn't feel this was financially possible, so I came up with a plan.

A few months before all our changes happened we were introduced to a great product that gave me energy I didn't know had. I knew that it could be a business, but I didn't now where to start. However, I knew who I could talk to learn more. So began my life as a network marketer.

Fast forward a few months, I had a new baby, I was homeschooling my three other daughters who were under six, and I was building a part-time business. Talk about no sleep. That's when the unthinkable happened, the economy crashed in Alberta, and my husband was eventually laid off.

Like so many families, we struggled to find work for him. It took us five months to get him a new job. I thank God every day that I came up with that plan for our family. My part-time business alleviated most of the stress during that turbulent time. Our family did not lose our home or vehicles like others that we knew. We spent those months he had off with our children, building my network marketing business, and sharing our experiences with others.

Through the years, I aligned myself with amazing mentors. Individuals that taught me and supported me. It was from them I learned how important it is to be coachable. To be the best you must learn from the best, don't try to reinvent the wheel. Do what they tell you to do because they have learned from their mistakes. I was encouraged to read books by Dale Carnegie, John C Maxwell, and Napoleon Hill. I attended live events like GoPro and listened to Todd Falcone. Whenever I took my children to appointments in the city, I listened to empowering podcasts from amazing people in business.

Spending this valuable time on myself gave me more confidence. I was able to interact with others on a much deeper level. I made connections that turned into friendships that I maintain even today.

I remember the day one of my mentors approached me, asking me to interview some of the women in Zija on her internet radio show. I think it was one of the most terrifying requests I've ever received. Even more so than when I went skydiving.

I don't remember what I said during those first few shows, but it did get better. The more amazing women I talked with and learned from, the more inspired I became.

Homeschooling my daughters also brought a lot of inspiration to my life, seeing the world through their eyes, learning and growing with them. I remember thinking, "Wouldn't it be a great idea to find other women outside of Zija and interview them too?"

My vision was to create a database of women talking about their personal journeys to share with my daughters. That was the start of my radio, show: Interviewing the Divas.

I spent time online searching for amazing women I felt would inspire the people listening to the show. Most of the women who came on the show were looking for new ways to make others aware of their personal businesses. It was an incredible opportunity for both of us to introduce the idea of the show to others.

All of our shows were recorded, and I promoted them on my social media pages. Many of my guests did the same. As time went by I also shared my story in magazines, and my viewership for the show went up, as did the number of women interested in being interviewed.

Homeschooling my girls and a trip to Mexico provided an experience that made me see the world differently. Together, they led me to rethink the show's purpose. My vision expanded to helping social entrepreneurs create positive changes in the world!

That led me to a new name and hashtag: #DivasThatCare. Our show is evolving into more than just women and their businesses. It reaches farther and goes deeper, asking what is crucial to my guests on a soul level. Along with their business, we now talk about causes and charities these brilliant women are involved with. We empower today's listeners but also future listeners.

I have developed a platform of recorded shows on www.divasthatcare.com that my guests can share and that my daughters can listen to in future years. These women are so inspirational. They are truly making a difference.

This summer I have a book coming out, and its mission is to support, inspire, and engage a community of committed women by offering ideas and strategies on how they can work together to make the world a better place. Not just for themselves but also for future generations.

Angela Goodyear Sellars

Angela is a life stylist coach who helps others to be empowered the way she has learned to empower herself through self-love. She strives to help build a connection between inner beauty and outer beauty. She believes that if you love yourself, love will flow out into the other areas, resulting in a more enriched life.

Angela lives in Newfoundland, Canada with her wonderful husband and her amazing son, who have both been so supportive in her endeavors.

Find Angela online:

www.naturalroadtowellness.com
https://www.facebook.com/naturalroadtowellness/
angela@naturalroadtowellness.com

Chapter 13

What Do You See When You Look in The Mirror?

By Angela Goodyear Sellars

It was the fall of 2014, and I was standing in front of the mirror feeling paralyzed with fear; horrified by what was looking back at me. I didn't have one kind word to say to myself, and I knew at that moment that I didn't love the person in the mirror. In my reflection, I saw my hair was breaking and falling out rapidly, I was missing eyelashes on my left eye. There was a cracked tooth in my smile, and I was haggard looking from a combination of exhaustion and poor nutrition. Worst of all were the scars imprinted on my body due to allergic contact dermatitis. Just days before this I was told that I had developed an autoimmune condition and my body was attacking itself by becoming allergic to anything and everything it had repeated exposure to. With my profession as a hairstylist, it happened to be the enormous load of environmental toxins that I was exposed to every day. I believe it was triggered from my body being depleted and the long hours of burning the candle at both ends. Standing in front of the mirror was a nightmare but as the days, months, and even years went by, it became my blessing, a beautiful gift. What message did I receive that day while I was looking in the mirror?

I was steering into the unknown with my eyes open, feeling paralyzed and emotionless. I saw nothing but darkness, no hope, no future, as I shook with the fear of trying to figure out who I was. I was left with only the words of the specialist ringing in my ears. It was as if my identity was stolen. My body was attacking me with allergies, and my world was never to be the same again. I was given no choice but to walk away from my career, my business and many of the people that I loved. It was confusing for me at first, but what I later realized was that while I was making everyone else beautiful I lost *my* beauty and this became my struggle.

As a hairstylist, I spent twenty-four years enhancing the beauty of others, and I loved it. Every day that I worked I was sure of my purpose, and I knew that I had a gift to see the beauty in every individual that I had the opportunity to touch. At work, I put myself together every day and walked out into the world as the full package. My life was portrayed as perfect, people became envious of me, and I came up against lots of jealousy.

My confidence always suffered because of this. I have always been so hard on myself and rarely ever felt proud of who I was. I always felt like I could do better than what I had accomplished. I spent my whole life needing others to boost me up, reassuring me that I was good, but I was attracting more jealousy and envious personalities. I continued to choose their thoughts over mine, and I stopped being authentic. I just wanted to be like everyone else. I continued to listen to them and believed everything they said about me. I cannot say it ever made sense, but at the end of the day, their opinions and views mattered to me. I began to believe that my uniqueness was causing my relationship struggles and I became embarrassed of my values.

My illness came on like a wild storm, but truly, it was destined to happen to me.

How did an allergy diagnosis change everything? It was December of 2013 when I noticed a rash on my arms. I kept putting off treating myself, and by the holidays, my arms were covered. I had recently purchased all sorts of nice short-sleeved tops, and I wasn't able to wear them that Christmas. I had to cover myself in long sleeve old clothing, once again feeling like I put everyone else first. Later, I discovered that the cheap black clothing I was choosing to wear was toxic and making me even sicker! These allergens forced me to spend the next year wearing nothing but one-hundred percent organic clothing. It looked quite different from my funky black clothing, big jewelry and high heel leather shoes that I wore daily. I became allergic to the metal in my scissors, which caused me to become allergic to the razors that I used to shave my legs and underarms. My world was turning upside down with allergies to hair products, makeup, metals, clothing, leather, and multiple food allergies. My *entire* world was changing. How can one live when their outer beauty is all they know, and their identity is being taken?

I am so grateful that I was given a wonderful doctor to help get me through this. She gave me a book called *When the Body Says No* by Dr. Gabor Maté. I read the stories in this book, and it helped me realize that I was a workaholic. My doctor said to me, "If you want to live a long life, you have to make changes, and if you want to live a short life then you can keep doing what you're doing." This is how I ended up looking into the mirror, feeling paralyzed while steering into the unknown darkness. "What now?" I asked myself. As I was standing in front of the mirror, I truly believe I received a message, but I had no idea that it would send me on the natural road to wellness that would heal my body. The message that I clearly received that day was, "Self-love will be your healing." After many days of thought, I set up a page on Facebook to share my journey with the world. I announced on that I would be falling in love with the person in the mirror, and the battle was on.

This was the exact post from that day:

This is the post that I have avoided for more than a week now. Why? Because it's why I got myself in this mess. It's been looking at me for a very long time, it's destroyed me; it has caused me my health, my career, and my true self. It started as a noise sitting on my shoulders at a young age talking to me, but then it convinced me it was true. True enough that it became my storm. It was the wildest adventure one could ever go on. So, scary that I woke up to my fears, my thoughts and my world came crashing down on October 18th. It was a storm, but was that the beginning I asked myself or was it the end? My body was saying enough is enough but was my mind going to give up? No, because the person in the mirror was me.

So, I made it my goal then, to fall in love with the woman in the mirror.

How? It's still a journey, but you will see how this person in the mirror got me bad and I have to say won the battle but the battle is still on, and my true self will win, and I will fall in love with the woman in the mirror in 2015.

I succeeded, and now I keep being asked the question, "How did you do it?" But my discovery led me to realize that it was never how I fell *in* love with the person in the mirror, but how I fell *out* of love with that person, and that's how we will all fall in love with ourselves. I had to look behind me, and that was scary to me but after lots of patience, questions and meltdowns, I finally found what I was looking for. I was not living my authentic self on a daily basis. I was being who others were molding me to be. I was feeling ashamed of my values, my true beliefs and my self-esteem were at their lowest. I managed to turn all this around through courage and self-love.

I believe if we are true to ourselves our smiles will become wider, our love tanks fuller, our health and beauty will shine brighter. Our relationships will become stronger, and our financial debt will disappear. I had to work on the four most important areas of my life, and I started with hiring a financial advisor. I became addicted to removing toxins in my home, and even when I went outside, I wouldn't walk on busy streets, only in nature. I brought yoga and meditation into my world as a practice, and I learned to breathe. I had to teach myself how to learn because in December of 2014 I was given an aptitude test and was told I had a learning disability. I always knew about it but I cried a river that day. I was so good at being a hairstylist, that education wasn't a priority for me anymore. But after all this, I learned that it does matter and many courses later I am now a proud life stylist coach who empowers others the same way I have empowered myself through self-love.

Even though I believe in the benefits of medication, I avoided it from the time I was diagnosed with my allergies up until now. I just believe that in my case, self-love was going to be my healing and needles were not an option for me. My specialist told me I needed to get a steroid injection once a month in order to live an everyday life with my allergies. I explained to him that I refused to put a Band-Aid on my problem! I set out to discover where my allergies came from and how I could eliminate them from my life through natural medicine.

So, what has been my medicine? Courage. The courage to wake up every morning and put my two feet on the floor. To be grateful that I was given a second chance and to have the courage to keep moving forward, believing that the obstacles that stand in front of me are making me stronger. It gives me the strength and stability to share my story with others and give them hope that their inner beauty is worth the fight.

My discovery is that when we make positive changes from within, our outside world will magically transform. I believe that when our inner beauty meets our outer beauty we are complete, we are whole and we are on Earth in our physical body being our authentic self. My memories of 2014 are very ripe, and I believe if I focus on the horrific times, I will receive more of those sleepless itchy nights, with hair loss and open sores. That is behind me, and now I am aware of the messages that my body sends me, so I take the time to listen. I have gone through this journey choosing the natural road to wellness inspired by my friend who later passed away of cancer. He wanted me to share with the world how awesome I was, so that's what I was inspired to do. I accomplished this through daily self-love rituals. I fell in love with myself and truly learned that we can heal with self-love. In one-year, I had no environmental or food allergies of any kind, and I have controlled my allergens instead of letting them control me.

My message I would love to share with the world is that self-love can be healing. Being true to your values and practicing self-love rituals can magically ripple out into the most important areas of your life. You will find that your health will improve, your relationships will become stronger and your debt will disappear. Material things will mean less, and your spiritual path will help you to look at obstacles differently. It will quiet your mind and help you move with intention, and this has been my biggest lesson. Loving myself has been my gift.

Now as I stand in front of the mirror, I think about the journey that helped me love the woman I have become. A woman that lives every day through her values and dreams. A woman that lives with gratitude and has finally begun loving life again. Now when I am faced with an obstacle, I coach myself the way I coach others, and the weight lifts off my chest. My life has become more abundant, my smile has become wider, and I have removed the mask that I have been wearing for such a long time. My wish to you is to take your mask off and have the world love you for being you.

Kathy Heinsohn

As a mind-body-soul coach, Kathy is an individual who can find beauty in anything from a horrible day to a sacred sunset. Kathy wants to live in a world where everyone is fully empowered in his or her divine birthright.

Kathy's been referred to as a 'word watcher,' and has been featured as a guest blogger, presenter, and speaker. Whether it's working with individuals one on one, on stage, or in group programs, it's her passion to empower others to get back in their own game of life and play full out.

Find Kathy online:

http://naturallykathy.com
https://www.instagram.com/kathyheinsohn/?hl=en
http://fb.me/naturallykathy

Chapter 14

The Road Back to My Heart

By Kathy Heinsohn

I can't believe I'm here again. My head hit the pillow, and the tears wouldn't stop falling (which was a big deal for someone who rarely allowed herself to cry). My heart was broken, and I couldn't find any sense of solace. *What's wrong with me? What more can I do? Why is God punishing me?* I was at a complete loss. I had always pictured myself at this stage of life with my own house (with a white picket fence and everything) surrounded with my kids running around, and a good husband. (I wasn't so naïve to expect prince charming, but at least someone who would tolerate my presence and was willing to trench through life together.) It felt like I was stuck in a living nightmare, watching all my friends and family living their dreams in full color. Dreams I had imagined for myself since I was a little girl. Here I was, living life in black and white, watching from the sidelines; exhausted, wishing, wanting, and praying to die.

My body felt like it was holding me hostage, where I was punished for eating the wrong thing, or left in major pain if I tried to move too much. I was continuously sick and completely worn down all the time. It took everything I had to get myself out of bed in the mornings after sleepless nights, but lying around all day wasn't an option (at least, that's not what my Boston terrier believed). I had to suck it up, let my furry friend out, and put myself aside (a constant habit). I also had to take care of my grandmother who was dealing with anxiety, depression (from losing her husband), and dementia (I swear if she asks me where the dog is one more time...I'm going to lose it). As if that weren't enough,

I had to be there for my mom (who was also in a frustrating and foreign place from where she had imagined she'd be). I was required to be the emotional support for everyone in my life, maintain the household, as well as work hours from home. I thought I would lose my mind from the sheer monotony of this never-ending carousel ride. "Get me off!" my heart screamed. Round and round and round I'd go, feeling like I was slowly suffocating from the never-ending heaviness inside.

I waited for the nightmare that was somehow my life, to end. My life. Those two words did not belong together. This was *not* my life! It couldn't be, could it? How did this happen? How did a grown woman in her thirties come to this place of helping support so many others in their dreams and lives that she somehow forgot to live her own? Who had *my* back while I was so busy having everyone else's? Who would keep me from falling apart when I was so busy holding others together?

I couldn't live my dreams; it wasn't allowed. If it was, that would mean I'd be free to breathe. Free to be myself, to express myself honestly without having a horrible misunderstanding or dismissal of what I thought and felt. I'd be free to be happy despite all the misery around me. I'd be able to dance to my own song, go hiking and biking like I did when I was a kid. I'd be able to run whenever I felt the desire, and I'd be able to move on and make something of my life. It seemed that I was forever stuck in this prison of a body with deep pain that was like a bad friend who stole everything from me. I couldn't believe that this was my reality.

The first time I found a heartstring pulling at me, nudging me to listen deeply, was when I was in college. I was twenty-years-old, beyond frustrated with visiting the doctor's office because I was sick (yet again), and nothing was working. My body had borne the brunt of my emotionally stuffing and holding everything together that it was spilling out in symptoms and disease everywhere. My immune system was shot, I was constantly exhausted, and it was commonplace to see blood every time I visited the bathroom. It was affecting my ability to work, concentrate in my classes, and even affected me going out into the world.

After years of this internal health crisis, I finally received a diagnosis of celiac disease (on top of a previous Hashimoto's diagnosis). It was at this time that I was reminded of my mom's brave journey through her health challenges and disease. By honoring her intuition and partaking of Mother Nature's gifts, she had found her own answers. The memory of her journey inspired me to purchase every book I could find on herbs, nutrition, alternative therapy, and mindset. I devoured these books much like my friends devoured pizza.

Gratefully, it started to help. I went on a thirty-day cleanse, and adopted a raw vegan diet. I added in green smoothies and threw out all the harsh chemicals in my house (in the form of cleaning supplies, beauty supplies, and plastics). I started to feel better almost immediately. I felt a glimpse of hope for the first time in my life of what it meant to be free.

When I was young, other people's expectations and responses had been the barometer I carried with me. I was always known as the 'perfect child' (even though I believed the opposite). It was life or death to keep track of what I thought I needed to do and be to measure up to everyone's expectations. If I could just try harder, do better, and keep them happy then they'd accept me. If I didn't cause any more pain than they already had, if I could just fix what's broken in them and make them comfortable and happy, my world would stop falling apart inside, and somehow, this constant dark black hole would leave me alone. If I could just be perfect, then everything would be…well, perfect. Except that it wasn't.

Years of starving myself, over exercising, controlling everything I put in my body, and forcing my emotions underground while putting on a happy face had carved its way deep inside.

Fast forward a few years, with me ending up back home with my mom (after my parents had divorced from thirty-two years of marriage), and I was having a pre-mid-life crisis. I realized I didn't want to do the career paths I had chosen (interior design, HR, then social work), and I couldn't for the life of me get a job. I had no clue what I was going to do when I grew up, as the once healing raw vegan diet was now creating other health issues.

I had nothing but time on my hands, and for someone who spent all her time trying not to feel, it was painstakingly miserable. This is the second time I had another heartstring tugging at me to listen. I remember pouring my heart out to God, which was a catch-twenty-two because God was the only person that knew all of me, but I also truly believed He didn't want me to be happy, that somehow I didn't deserve His love and acceptance. So I had always talked with God as if He were my best friend, but I never believed I was worth answering or getting anything in return. As

I poured my heart out to Him, I remember letting God know that I didn't want to be here anymore. I was done. I finally surrendered and gave in. I couldn't carry my life anymore.

It was in this space of surrender that I was finally ready and open to hear God's answer. For me, it came in the form of a book called *The Power of Infinite Love and Gratitude* by Dr. Darren Weissman. I couldn't leave the bookstore without it (which left me with 27 cents in my bank account). I read it all that evening and *knew* that it was going to change my life. I hopped online to read more about this incredible doctor. I found that he had the first of several modules to become a certified lifeline practitioner coming up in two weeks in Sedona, AZ. I didn't know *how* I was going to come up with the thousands to go; I just *knew* I was going to find a way. Miracle after miracle occurred and 13,000 dollars showed up along the way for me to travel, complete all the modules and earn my certification. I finally felt that I had come home — home to my heart.

From The Lifeline Technique® I discovered the power of infinite love and gratitude, the five basics of self-care (water, food, rest, exercise, and owning my own power), and how the subconscious and conscious mind works. I began an incredible, ever-unfolding journey of self-acceptance and healing of my soul (along with many of my disease symptoms, or dis-ease, which is really the body's lack of ease and harmony within itself). I learned to tune in and breathe into my feelings, not judge them, but allow the energy in motion (E-motion) to flow through me (not stuff, block, or resist them), and to use my feelings and symptoms as information into the inner workings of my mind. I learned to listen to my body and to what it needed (sometimes I still argue with it and tell it that it *needs* that cupcake or cheese, but it always disagrees).

I found greater love and compassion for others for where they're at and the experiences they have in life, and most importantly for myself (as I was great at extending love and compassion to others, but denied it to myself). We don't know what we don't know, and often, we're all walking around wounded from our family history of dysfunctional beliefs, traditions, and habits that we hope to better with each generation. It's all one giant ball of mess that somehow unravels into this crazy beautiful journey that somehow works, even in a dysfunctional way.

I learned that it's possible to release the dysfunctional and limiting BS (belief systems) that run our life. I now know that if we don't listen to the signals and strings that our heart is tugging at us to hear, our symptoms and disease speak louder, until we are forced to face them (which can sometimes be painful). My emotions and thoughts were stuffed in so tight, that my body couldn't help but erupt with hives, allergies, pain, and disease.

I see my symptoms of disease as one of the greatest mentors I've ever had. I have forgiven my body and the autoimmune symptoms I've experienced (and still sometimes experience) because I realize they were there to protect me, to help me look deep within, and to come home to myself. This has also helped me to truly find God. Not the God that I believed hated me deep down, or that I thought I had pissed off and could never be forgiven. My Father, the Creator of the Universe, knows me intimately and *loves* me unconditionally. He wants me to have joy and to know of His love.

I now appreciate that the beliefs and perceptions I grew up believing, were based on fear and protection, not my divine truth. The divine truth is that I am worthy and deserving of love and acceptance exactly as I am, that I do have a choice in each

125

experience. I choose love. This is a choice that comes only by conversing with my heart.

I learned how to be ok seeing others own their feelings and experiences, and that their symptoms, stress, and disease are coming from their own BS, which is divinely designed to protect them. Their experiences will also become their greatest mentor if they choose to learn from them.

Most importantly, I've learned what it was like to come home to the symphony of my heart. Since learning The Lifeline Technique®, I have whole-heartedly embraced it into my life, letting the power of infinite love and gratitude work miracles in all areas of my life. I have loved incorporating it and letting it unfold and morph into the bodywork and transformational coaching I do. The Lifeline Technique® has taught me to view symptoms of stress and disease as the individual's subconscious reacting out of protection. I am now able to help clients find freedom from disease and debilitating challenges such as anxiety, depression, addiction and PTSD so that they can find acceptance, peace, healing, and freedom.

While I would love to write that I'm happily married and living every dream I have ever imagined—I'm not there yet. I'm not perfect, but I'm ok with that now. I still get triggered, and I have flare-ups. Some days, I stuff things inside to keep the peace at home, and my body responds with food intolerances and creates a protection of fat to 'keep me safe' from what I perceive as a difficult environment. I seek to see the gift in this experience, and much awareness and healing have come as a result.

Being human, I bump into people who trigger my wounds and limiting beliefs. It's a daily choice of consciously choosing to question the beliefs to see if they're coming from a place of love or fear. Sometimes the fear wins. However, as I tune in, the time it takes me to shift is hours, minutes, or seconds, compared to the weeks, months, and years I lived with before. I have a new awareness in life that allows me to get to the heart of the matter quickly and easily.

My challenges look different now. Instead of believing I'll never be enough, and feeling as if I need to fix everything so that I'm loved and accepted, I purposely look for the gift in every experience. I am truly humbled and grateful to help others find their own heart's voice and to facilitate big shifts and breakthroughs with clients, family, and friends. I love witnessing miracles and seeing their lives change for the better (myself included). I'm in love with the life I'm creating and I'm excited to see how my journey continues to unfold.

Infinite love and gratitude to your perfectly imperfect journey, and mine.

Julie Kapuschak

Julie Maye is a twenty-two-year-old girlfriend, Mom and kitty-owner. She is known for her work as a medium, energy healer and spiritual coach, as well as for being a published author and freelance writer. When Julie isn't writing or sharing time with her family, she is either napping or enjoying the sunshine. If you can't find her snuggled up in bed or walking around the neighborhood, then she's probably at the garden center. Julie loves tea, and all things spiritual and positive. Despite having a difficult life, she still believes in infusing each day with positivity and passion.

Find Julie online:

http://www.faerysage.com
http://www.fb.me/faerysage
hello@juliemaye.com

Chapter 15

Life Won't Stop, and Neither Will I

By Julie Kapuschak

Almost twenty-two years ago at the time of writing this book, I was born in Vancouver, B.C. My life as I knew it at was perfect. I was an innocent baby born to a young mother and father in their late teens. The time, as I was told, was 5:50 pm. That was the first and the last time that my life was remotely 'normal' and picture perfect. From there, things rapidly deteriorated.

When I was just four-months-old, I was rushed into the clinic with a broken collarbone, bruising on my wrist and a burn on the end of my nose from a lit cigarette. While no one owned up to the incident, there was one person who I am certain was responsible. That person's silence changed the course of my life—forever.

That incident led to child protective services removing me from my home and placing me in temporary foster care. At that point, there were two options: my biological parents could choose my adoptive family, or I would be placed in the system. My biological parents chose to adopt me to my great aunt (Mom) and great uncle (Dad). Although life growing up was not easy, I strongly believe it was the best possible outcome for me. Still, even though I was adopted into the family, the feud over the incident caused my new parents and myself to be isolated from a large portion of our family.

Many things in my life led to my partying habits in my early teen years. A narcissistic mother, a constant wondering of where I came from, and bullying both at home and in school caused me to have depression and anxiety. I self-medicated through drinking, smoking, and using drugs from the age of thirteen. At the time, it was the only way I could find relief from my pain. Looking back, I'm honestly not ashamed of the person I was throughout my teenage years. However, if you asked me two years ago, I would have never admitted it.

In the middle of my teen years, I got into a relationship with a boy who was toxic. He was narcissistic, arrogant, and truly an unsafe person to be around. I was addicted to the thrill that he brought to my life. Together we explored our surroundings, went off-roading, stayed in his parents' cabin, camped, and spent almost every waking minute together. We were together an entire year. Despite how dreamy the relationship seemed, it wasn't. We fought often, and although he was unaware, I cheated on him frequently. I don't have a good reason as to why I did, other than the fact that I was an unhappy person and I wanted everyone else to be unhappy with me.

About a year into our relationship, I brought him over to one of my ex-boyfriend's houses. This was around the time I was getting back into drugs after being mostly sober for the duration of our relationship. I would often sneak drugs into our relationship and hide them from him. At this point, I had tried to break up with him numerous times, but he made it virtually impossible by refusing to let me leave. He had developed an almost stalker-like mentality. I thought the only way out was to get him to leave me.

My plan was deeply flawed. After we had left my ex's house to head back to my boyfriend's house, he got rude. He didn't know that I had cheated on him at my ex's house, but I think he suspected something. Along the way, I said I would pull off the highway, and his dad could come and get him. He said he would throw my keys into a field and make me "Deeply regret it." I was scared, so I kept driving. We arrived at his house, and he was screaming at me in my truck. I started screaming back, but he wasn't listening so I got right up in his face. My exact words were "If you can't talk to me with respect, get out of my truck!"

The next moment was a blur, but I remember it clearly, if that makes any sense? Time seemed to freeze as he dove over the console and wrapped his hands around my throat. He pushed so hard that my head went down onto the seat and my entire body was shoved under the steering wheel. I couldn't breathe, and I wasn't sure what I was supposed to do. I had to get out and run, but my phone was dead, and I had nothing to get away with. I started digging in the door for something to use as a weapon to try to defend myself with. Suddenly, he let go and sat back into his seat. From what I could tell, we were both stunned.

The argument *still* didn't stop. He held me captive for the next eight hours. I tried to leave, but he threw my truck into park as I was driving. He threatened that if I left it would be worse. He went from fuming angry and aggressive to begging me to stay. Whenever I would try to leave or trick him so I could go, he would transition from pleading with me to being aggressive. I felt like I was trapped in a horror movie I couldn't escape from. Unsure of what to do, and too tired to drive the two hours' home, I went to sleep in his bed. He tried to cuddle up to me, but I shoved him away. The feelings I experienced that night were terrifying. As I write this, I can feel the memory of them haunting me and the pain creeping back into my mind. To say I am healed would be a lie. I still struggle daily.

I went home the next morning after telling his parents what had happened. I had to work, but luckily, I had told my colleagues about what had occurred the night before. They looked out for me when he came into my workplace and handed me a bunch of flowers—with a grin spread across his face as if nothing had happened.

He biked for six hours to get there; just to pretend nothing had gone on between us the night before. I let him sleep in my truck, then called his parents and drove him back to my house where he was welcomed to sit on the porch until his dad got there. My dad had no idea what had happened yet; I was too scared to tell anyone. How could I? I felt like it was all my fault for letting my guard down around him.

We broke up, and I resumed drinking and taking drugs. My frame of mind made it seem like it was a good idea to start seeing him again just a few months later. My friends all worked hard to get me to stay away from him, but I refused to listen. What hit home for me was when he said he would do it all over again because "A woman should never disrespect her man." That was the last time I saw him, aside from the times that he stalked my house, driving by late at night and looking directly at me as I sat smoking out front.

After that, my addictions got worse. I smoked almost a pack-and-a-half of cigarettes every day, I used drugs a lot more, and I drank more than I ever had just to numb myself. I would take virtually anything that would keep my mind from wandering back to that place. It didn't matter that when I sobered up, it went there even more, because as far as I knew I would never need to sober up and therefore everything would be fine. I would never have to think about it. Only, I did. I thought about it a lot.

When I wasn't drinking or popping pills, I was at work. Work was my other outlet to keep myself from thinking about anything else. The smartest move I ever made was leaving the job I'd worked at when I was dating that boy, and finding work elsewhere.

It was in another job that I met the love of my life. A few weeks into my job in a department store, I did a manifesting visualization practice to attract true love into my life. After so many undesirable situations all had ended by an abusive partner, I wanted to know what it was like to feel like the girls in the movies. I wanted to be loved by my own prince charming.

About a week later, just after my eighteenth birthday, I met Toby. He was working in a different department, and I was anything but attracted to him. He did not fit the 'bad boy' look I generally went for, and maybe that drew me in even more. We started spending a lot of time together, and before I knew it, we were dating. I wish I could say it was all easy from there, but it wasn't. I was still heavily damaged from my past, and I didn't know how to be in a healthy and loving relationship.

I quit drinking and smoking, and stopped using drugs. Toby and I had a lot of fun spending time together goofing around, and getting to know each other. However, when I went through my downwards spirals, they were dark. I would scream, hit him, throw things, and completely lose it. I blamed him for my negative emotions. He received the hate that I felt toward a large portion of my family and my exes, especially the abusive ones.

Fortunately, for me, he stuck it out. Somehow, he knew what I was going through, and he was able to truly see the real me in it all. He held on tight and promised me he was never going anywhere, even when I tried to kick him out and break up with him on countless occasions. I never felt worthy of him, and I didn't want him to stick around to be treated so poorly by someone as damaged as I was.

Somewhere in it all, I found myself again. My anger dialed down, I regained control, and I healed from a large portion of it all. Although I was still hurting from the memories, I wasn't feeling controlled by them anymore. I felt like I was me again. My positivity was restored, my happiness was brought back, and my life was filling up with purpose and passion again.

A year into our relationship, Toby and I got pregnant with our daughter. We were both excited, as we had secretly been trying for a baby since the beginning. Somehow, even under all of the chaos and damage, we both knew that we were destined to be together forever. I was nineteen when I got pregnant, and twenty when she was born. It was the happiest day of my life, despite many family members trying to take that away from us. For once, I knew where I belonged, and I felt zero doubt. I looked into the eyes of my innocent daughter, but at the same time, I was seeing through the eyes of my innocent self, twenty years prior.

The feeling of bliss was short lived. When my daughter was just one-month-old, my mom was diagnosed with stage four terminal cancer. Toby and I were celebrating our third anniversary on November 12th, 2015. My mom came home with the news. In an instant, I became both a new mom and a full-time caregiver. I didn't know how to manage it all, but I truly believe I did the best I could. I took care of my daughter every waking minute and spent as much time with my mom as possible. At the time, we still lived in my parents' house, so we were available at a moment's notice. What I once thought was a curse, turned out to be a blessing.

On June 6th, 2016 my mom passed away. It was four days before my twenty-first birthday, and I strongly believe that she didn't want me to start a new year without her. It was the worst day of my life, above all other experiences. Although I handled everything better than I ever could've possibly imagined, I also struggled. It was the first major incident I endured without the assistance of drugs and alcohol, and although I had no desire to use in order to numb myself, I also had no coping methods to help me. It was a long few months of finding myself again, and I'm not even sure I fully have, yet.

Since my mom passed, I started a new business, and then another one. My original one aligned more with the assistance I needed around healing at the time, and my current one aligns perfectly with who I truly am in life. I am now a medium, an energy healer, a spiritual coach, and an author. I use my gift to communicate with my mom and others, on a regular basis, and it has assisted me greatly in life. Despite it all, I am so blessed to be where I am today.

This ride hasn't been easy. I still haven't experienced a moment as innocent and blissful as the one on the day that I was born. I don't know if I ever will again. However, I have come to peace with that. Each day as I watch my daughter grow, I am reminded of the innocence of life, and I am fueled by the desire to give her all that I never had. I realize every tragedy that ever happened was a blessing in one way or another, and I am passionate about my ability to carry through, despite it all. I don't know where I am going from here, and I don't have a beautiful fairy tale ending to give you, but I do know that life goes on, and sometimes that's all the motivation that you need.

Diana Madrigal

Diana is a certified professional coach, writer, and wife to a wonderful husband. She is a mother of two smart boys and one strong girl. She has been in customer service for over fifteen years working in retail, government, and private sectors. Diana has been a licensed loan officer and real estate agent for over a decade. She loves makeup artistry, cooking, reading, listening to music, and hiking. Her true passion lies in creative writing and life coaching. As an introverted coach, Diana has found joy in helping others find their personal power and face challenges with grace and self-awareness.

Find Diana online:

http://www.empowermentdiana.com/
https://www.facebook.com/introvertsempowerment
https://instagram.com/introvertsempowerment

Chapter 16

Finding Myself After Losing It All

By Diana Madrigal

When I attempted suicide, I was desperate for a breakthrough. Although, I was looking for an external one, based on outside factors and catalysts. At that moment, I could've never imagined that the real breakthrough was to be had within myself.

I was born into this world on September 23rd, 1986. The first day of fall; I always thought that was such a beautiful date to be born on. Now, I know that every single day, every single moment is beautiful; even during the darkest times. We can only know the light if we also know darkness. I grew up in southern California, where my parents raised me along with three brothers and two sisters. Growing up, I loved to read and write; I loved to tell stories. I was a shy, introverted child so I grew up to be self-conscious with a low self-esteem. I always felt different; like I didn't belong. I kept searching for that sense of belonging and acceptance throughout my teenage years. Never loving myself, but wishing with all my might that if someone else loved me, it might fill the void in my heart.

On October 31st, 2005 I met my oldest son's father. I had just turned nineteen, and he was twenty-two. We fell in love quickly. By December of that year, we eloped, and when my parents found out, they were understandably upset. They did not like him; they had higher hopes for me. They wanted me to go to college, become a wealthy professional so I could help them get out of poverty. Instead, I fell in love, got married and moved out. I quit community college but kept my office job. My mom stopped talking to me for about six months, which hurt me terribly. Around that time, when we had just reconnected I found out I was pregnant. Again, my parents were not happy. Not because they wouldn't love the baby, but because they felt my son's dad didn't deserve me. My mom once told me I was her precious diamond. If only I had understood and believed her, I would have saved myself so much heartache.

When my son was around eight-months-old, I recall his dad being on the couch and him telling me he was starting to feel depressed (he had felt depression in his teen years). I was worried about him; I kept thinking of how I could help him or find support. A week later, he told me he wanted a divorce. He said I was overweight, lazy, and that he deserved a wife that looked good and that he'd be proud to be with. My already low self-esteem became non-existent after that moment. All I knew was to get mad and defensive; we fought and argued—so I went to stay with my parents for about a month. During that month, one of his friends passed away. He called me the night of the funeral and told me seeing his late friend's wife crying for her husband made him realize he wanted to make things work between us.

I returned to what I can only describe as hell-on-earth. I don't blame him though; I had a huge role to play in creating that hell. Everything I said, did or didn't do bothered him. My resentment made me angry and extremely short-fused. We were roommates who couldn't stand each other, but I kept convincing myself that if I just fought hard enough, I could get through to him. That I could make him see and understand that I loved him more than anything.

Then came the jealousy, I noticed we were no longer getting a cell phone bill in the mail. I became more vigilant. I noticed he never left his cell phone unattended; he even hid it at night. He'd go as far as taking out the SIM card and hiding it in an entirely different place to where he hid the phone. He had started going out to bars with his friends, staying out very late, and then would come home drunk. I remember crying to him once asking him what he was looking for out there, that his family was at home. I felt so alone and isolated. The jealousy and paranoia drove me crazy. It was all I would think about, imagining scenarios and hypothetical situations. We'd get into huge fights to the point of him shoving me into the wall, pushing me down to the floor, or pinning me down to control me when I'd flip out on him.

I finally left our house in August of 2008, but we kept being with each other and sharing custody of our son. Even after I moved out, I had hope that it would all pass, mainly because he kept that glimmer of hope alive. However, things just kept getting worse.

At that time I had lost my job, we were losing our house to the bank, and he started the divorce proceedings. I felt so confused; I was always in a fog trying to make sense of how my life had gotten to that point. I repeatedly asked myself where I had gone wrong? What had I done to deserve all these bad things happening to me? It was like a disease that consumed my whole existence. One day I just drove and kept driving until it got dark. I called my parents and told them that I wasn't coming home that night because I needed to be alone and to make sure my son was ok. I slept at a hotel and the next day when I went home to my parents' place my mom chastised me and told me my dad had said I was selfish and a bad mother for doing that. It hurt me so much to hear her say those things to me. I felt like a failure. I felt so much guilt; it was all I could think of for a week.

That weekend I went to our house where my son's dad was still staying. I walked up to the room, and the door was slightly ajar. He was lying on the bed talking on the phone and pleasuring himself. I completely lost it. I burst through the door, we started arguing, and a huge fight ensued. In the middle of the fight, he just walked away from me.

I had a breakdown. I remember feeling like I was no longer in control. I was just along for the ride. It felt like watching a movie; so surreal. In a desperate attempt to make him pay for everything he was putting me through, I locked myself in the bathroom. I dug through the medicine cabinet and found some painkillers from my cesarean section. This bottle was the answer. It would put an end to all this pain that ripped me apart. I took a handful of pills and washed them down with faucet water. Then, I had an even better idea. I ran to the kitchen and grabbed a knife. This would be much faster, I decided. I must've grabbed the dullest one we had because I felt every single tooth on that small, serrated knife. I could only draw a little blood, but my tendons were on fire as I cut right above my wrist tattoo of his name. *How fitting,* I said to myself. I lay on the floor sobbing, feeling like my whole world was crashing down on me; coming to a melodramatic end.

Growing up with low self-esteem and having no idea how to love myself, I was already at a disadvantage when my young marriage ended. Losing everything at once was a pivotal point, and it's no wonder I reacted the way I did. It wasn't 'just' about a man. It was a loss of identity and a fear of the unknown. I was overcome with feelings of guilt, failure, and a genuine conviction that I was unworthy and unlovable. My identity as a person was solely based on being the wife and mother I had dreamed I'd be since I was a little girl. My self-worth was entirely dependent on his approval of the roles I played for him. I never thought about what made me happy, what my personal future might hold, or what made me who I was or wanted to be. When your identity is completely shattered, there's an overwhelming sense of loss. I felt unworthy and unlovable because I figured I couldn't make my marriage work, so there must be something inherently wrong with me. I blamed myself for everything.

As I lay there crying, I told myself my son would be much better off without me. He deserved better than me, I was sure. "He won't even remember any of this," I muttered to myself. A few minutes later, he came back, realizing I had locked myself in, he banged on the door and ordered me to open it. I refused, so he kicked a hole in it and opened it. He saw the knife and prescription bottle and screamed, "What did you do!?" To which I replied that it didn't matter.

He called my oldest sister who lived nearby, and she rushed over. She came into the room and asked what was going on. I completely went off on her; I told her everyone felt the right to judge me and thought their lives were so perfect, but they weren't. They were just as fucked up as mine. She was speechless and began to cry; she turned to him and told him to call the police. The police and ambulance arrived a few minutes later. Most of what I remember after that are just snippets; like getting in the ambulance, arriving at the hospital and being transferred to the behavioral health wing. I stayed there for the mandatory seventy-two-hour hold.

During my stay at behavioral health, I immersed myself in books, trying not to think about what I had tried to do. I was remorseful and ashamed. I also realized I didn't belong there. I wasn't crazy; I had just gone through a challenging situation and made a huge mistake, but I deserved a second chance at life. My mom came to visit me, and so did my son's dad. He held my hand, and I thought everything was going to be ok. Upon my release, I was referred to a free counseling clinic where I went to talk to a therapist and was prescribed anti-depressants. I took them for a month or so but hated the way they made me feel, and I felt I couldn't properly care for my son while taking them. My son's dad and I didn't get back together; our marriage was over for good.

I knew things had to change. I didn't want to feel like a failure day in and day out. I was tired of being tired. Hitting rock bottom made me realize I wanted to keep going. With time, I came to understand that my son did deserve a better life *with* me. That I did deserve to live the life I had once envisioned.

It took years and a lot of inner work to improve the relationship within myself. By surrounding myself with the people that cared about me, I was able to become a healthier, happier version of myself. I learned that only I could give my son the best home, life, and mother. The day I realized that I had to accept the apology I would never receive, freed my soul. Not because the other person deserved it, but because I merited inner peace. Resentment wasn't hurting them; it was only hurting *me*. Letting go of anger and what didn't serve me made more room in my life for all the good things that were out there for me. It multiplied my gratitude so that I can enjoy what matters to me like my family, my authenticity, my creativity, and living my purpose. Without this experience, I may have never known how strong I was. I am thankful for the difficult times I have gone through because they taught me these powerful lessons. I've made it my purpose to help others live the life they too envision. I believe that through my story, others in similar situations can find their inner-strength, self-love, and overcome any challenge.

Evelyne Nyairo

Evelyne is a socially conscious innovator and the driving force behind the luxurious all-natural skincare line, Ellie Bianca.

Ellie Bianca is a passion project inspired by Evelyne's daughter, the company's namesake. It's a women's' empowerment venture designed to "Heal not just the skin, but the soul." Ellie Bianca is a beacon of hope and global connection.

Having achieved her Master's degree in Environmental Management, Evelyne provides strategic planning on high-profile projects worldwide and has held many energy sector leadership positions.

Find Evelyne online:

https://store.elliebianca.com

Chapter 17

Courage is Built by Hard Work and Dreams that Scare the Crap Out of You

By Evelyne Nyairo

The day I discovered I was pregnant I could practically hear the sound of my dreams shattering. I was twenty-three-years-old and close to finishing my undergraduate degree at a Canadian university half a world away from where I'd grown up in Kenya. My whole life, I'd planned to travel the world after school and then go to graduate school and begin to build a career I could be proud of. I certainly never planned to raise a child alone.

I spent the next nine months terrified, often hiding under the covers afraid to face the day, and crushed under the weight of my broken dreams.

When I held my daughter for the first time, everything changed.

As I cradled her tiny body, I felt an incredible warmth. I had intended to name my daughter Bianca, but as I watched her gazing at the world with wisdom in those bright young eyes, I decided to call her Eliana. It means, my God has answered me. My fears melted away as her presence filled me with comfort.

Ellie's entire future depended on my decisions. From that moment forward, I decided I would do whatever it took to give her every opportunity in life. We all need a deeper meaning, a *why* for doing whatever we dedicate our lives to. Ellie was never a handicap to my success; she immediately became my *why*.

From her first day on this planet, Ellie taught me I could not afford to opt-out of my life. It was time for me to throw off the covers and be courageous. Being courageous doesn't mean I'm not afraid. No way. In fact, I go out of my way to find challenges that intimidate me. Early on, the only way to survive was to face my fears. Now, setting goals that challenge and even scare me is what urges me forward.

Ellie was my *why* for being courageous, but I had to be my own *how*. I'd always been driven to be successful, and hard work doesn't scare me. Good thing, too, because nothing was easy in those early days. I'd graduated with my Bachelor of Science months before Ellie was born. I stayed on maternity leave for three months, but I was too restless to spend a whole year at home. I enrolled in more university courses, this time in public health, but soon learned it wasn't the career path for me.

I had a burning desire to keep things moving in my life and find my calling—but there was a problem. I hadn't taken any student loans while in school, which meant I'd sometimes leaned on my credit card. I was trying to repay credit card debt while raising my child as a single parent and making $13 an hour in a lab. I had become an expert at ignoring credit card bills.

I craved the stability my mom had created for my siblings and me. It gave us so many opportunities growing up. My untenable financial situation was freaking me out. It became clear to me I could either let that fear paralyze me, or I could do something about it. That meant doing something I'd never done before. So I started with the first step.

I gathered my courage (and my bills) and began tracking my debts and my expenditures. Seeing those numbers on paper was intimidating, but it also gave me control. Now that I knew the numbers, I could do something about it. My financial management became meticulous. I recorded everything, down to the 25 cents it cost for an hour of parking.

Slowly, I pushed my bank account back into balance. Slowly, I saved enough to buy Ellie and me our first house, and our first true stability since I'd discovered I was pregnant.

As I started to establish myself in my career as an environmental scientist, I asked to be transferred to my company's head office in another city. It meant moving across the province and re-establishing myself and Ellie, but it was an opportunity to grow within the company to take on international projects and more responsibility. That wasn't the only way I was planning for the long-term. Ellie was two when I applied to graduate school. Another intimidating goal.

Remember I said that I'm not afraid of hard work? Earning my Master's degree was one of my biggest tests. I got through the coursework fine and even managed to complete the on-campus portion of my semester in another province thanks to the help of friends, loved ones, and my church.

Then it was time to write my thesis. It happened to come up around the same time I was saving up for a downpayment for a new house. My dad had instilled in me that there is no such thing a genius, just people who work hard. My mom had taught me that determination and persistence would get you success. I took this to heart. When people hear I am a single mother, they immediately assume it's an insurmountable obstacle to my dreams. "Poor Evelyne, she must have it hard." Yes, it was tough—it still is—but in no way did it mean that my daughter would ever have less opportunity than any other child. If I was willing to work for it, I could achieve it.

I got a paper route to earn enough money for my down payment while I completed my thesis. For six months, my days went something like this: I'd wake up at midnight and head to the newspaper depot to prepare the papers for other carriers before delivering my own routes. I'd get home around 5 am, shower and sleep for a couple of hours. Then I'd get up again, put on my suit and drive downtown to my energy sector job as a senior project manager for all of Canada from 8 am until 4:30 pm. After work, I shut my office door, and it was thesis time. Then it was home to dinner, put Ellie to bed, grab a few hours' sleep, and repeat. (I don't like coffee, but during this time, I learned to love a chai latte with a double shot of espresso.)

Ellie, my *why*, was my constant inspiration. I did what I did both to support our lives and to set an example for her. She would ask me, "Mommy, how many chapters do you have?" Urging me on page by page. On the days when it was hardest when I didn't want to do it for myself, I could at least be accountable to her.

When I conquered my thesis, I joined many other students by graduating into a deep recession. Nevertheless, I felt energized by the prospect of striking out on my own. When my employer started making cuts, I stepped away from the security I'd come to rely on and took another scary leap.

On my first day as a self-employed environmental consultant, I was elated. It's an amazing feeling to be responsible only to you, to have limitless freedom and your motivation guiding you.

Then, reality hit.

That first day, I checked my email. There was absolutely nothing in my inbox. I had no idea where to start. I went back to bed and cried. Not my finest moment. This can happen when we set goals and dream dreams that are so bold that they scare the crap out of us.

I had to remember that the courage to achieve our goals does not come all at once. To build boldness, we just have to start. I think of it like running. I love running so much I'll run up hills on a minus 20-degree day. In that moment, with the wind piercing through my jacket and frosting my cheeks, it can feel pretty rough. Each stride is training for the next one, and it's all building to a bigger achievement. I may not know how to get to the end yet, but I know how to take the first step.

On day two, I made a rule: don't stop working until I've made ten prospecting calls. From that day, I used my network, took every available opportunity and began to build my consultancy, one-step at a time.

One of the best things I did for myself as I built my business was to find my cheerleaders; trusted people who totally had my back. For me, one of those cheerleaders was my friend Andy. I'd proven my quality of work to him, so when his employer had a significant project, he called me. That project provided stability for the next five years, giving me a little extra space to dream big.

There were still days when I felt like staying under the covers. Those days, I needed a little help, so I wrote a contract with myself. It said, *I'm a courageous woman who inspires others to lead a more fulfilling life.* It was something I had learned about myself from Ellie. Reading those words was a reminder to keeping showing up to my own life.

Ten years after Ellie was born, I sat down with a financial planner and asked him what I had to do to retire by age forty-five. He gave me a really big number and then told me that was how much money I had to save every month if I wanted to retire by forty-five. I needed a lot of money in the bank to be able to do it.

That number is too big, I thought—but if your goals aren't intimidating, they're not big enough. Just like when I had paid off my student debt or saved money from my paper route for a down payment, now that I had the facts, I could start making decisions—and sacrifices—to get to my goal. Every decision I made had to align with my new savings and earnings goal. I never stepped into a mall. I reverted to my early debt-erasing days of tracking every cent I spent.

I'd asked my sister to open my bank statements for me while I was on a work trip overseas sometime later. When I got home, she broke the news. "Evelyne, I can't believe your bank balance. What on Earth have you been doing?"

I was almost as shocked as she was. I had stuck with my program and arrived at the finish line way ahead of schedule. I'd saved enough to retire by age thirty-five. *Do I retire at thirty-five and spend the rest of my life coasting? Surely, my life to this point, as an immigrant, a single mother, and a successful business woman could be helpful to other people in some way,* I thought. I searched for the next opportunity.

I was in a mango field in Chad, in Central Africa during a work trip, when I began to see my next way forward. A woman and her children were climbing trees to harvest fresh mangoes, and I was eager to buy some of the ripe fruit from a fellow female entrepreneur.

When I took out my money to pay the woman, my guide stopped me. "Pay the man," I was told. It was customary. There was a man present, sure. He was sitting on the sidelines watching the women and children work. I paid him, but my mind was racing. I realized how important gender issues were to me. I'm an African woman, and could so easily have been in this woman's position, laboring with a limit on my opportunities. As a woman in engineering, I'm frequently asked to check things with my boss; rarely do they expect me to *be* the boss.

I knew then that I wanted to do something to raise up women and children and support their businesses and education. The next day, I returned and bought more mangoes. This time, I paid the woman directly, with my mind on the future, not tradition.

My newest business venture, Ellie Bianca, was born.

Ellie Bianca is a social enterprise that bears by daughter's name. It is a celebration of what I went through to become successful and a company that champions other women.

Through five years of research and development, my team and I developed the Ellie Bianca luxury skin care line derived from African shea butter and oil that is sustainably and fairly sourced from women-run co-ops. Our long-term goal includes profit-sharing with the women who supply our shea, hibiscus and other natural resources. For now, we sponsor education for African girls and boys with the goals of instilling opportunity, business skills and respect for gender equality.

Today, my days are spent in our lab, putting my chemistry knowledge to the test to develop and refine our products while designing our storefront based on my teenage daughter's designs. My next goal for Ellie Bianca is to create a billion-dollar luxury skin care brand within an extremely competitive industry.

I'm a courageous woman. I know what I want. Now I just have to go work for it.

Dr. Erin Oksol

Dr. Erin is a clinical psychologist and business success coach. In addition to her private practice, she coaches business owners and entrepreneurs both in-person and virtually. She is an expert in cognitive-behavioral psychology and is published in ten peer-reviewed psychology journals and books. With over fifteen years of clinical experience, Dr. Erin shares her expertise with others to help them create significant positive change, both personally and professionally. She is a professional speaker and enjoys inspiring people to live their best life. Erin and her husband, Garth, live in Reno, NV with their three children, Grace, Emily, and Zachary.

Find Erin online:

https://www.facebook.com/thepsychologyofmission/
drerinoksol@thepsychologyofmission.com

Chapter 18

Progress, Not Perfection

By Dr. Erin Oksol

"You're too pretty to be in jail," she said as we waited in line for the nurse to dispense our medication. I thought of many other ways I could complete that sentence that would be more fitting and accurate. I was too smart to be in jail. I have a Ph.D. in clinical psychology. I have too great a marriage to be in jail. I am married to what I still believe is the perfect guy, or as close as one can get this side of heaven. I'm too blessed to be in jail. I have three stunningly beautiful and voraciously smart children: Grace, Emily, and Zachary. I'm too privileged to be in jail. I have two nice cars, a cute dog, and a gorgeous home. I'm too loved to be in jail. I have tons of friends who love me and support me. So why was I here? How did this happen to a good girl like me? Pain. That's the common denominator. It is non-discriminatory and doesn't care about your socio-economic status, much less how pretty you might be. Pain. It's the common entry point into depression, addiction, and sometimes jail.

That was in 2012. I woke up in a drunk tank in the county jail wearing jeans that were covered in my own vomit, not knowing if I had killed anyone and *certainly* not knowing my future fate. Well, I didn't 'wake up'—that's a euphemism we alcoholics call 'came to.' It's another way of saying I finally came out of my blackout after drinking an insane amount of alcohol and driving my minivan around town. I thank my God above that he spared me and everyone else on the roads that day and that I did not physically harm anyone. I thank my God that I have fully restored my relationships with my husband and children and that we are all healthy and thriving.

So how does one go from being at their personal rock bottom to being one of the happiest people they know in five short years? From doing crunches on my bunk and lunges in my 10X10 concrete jail cell to completely transforming my inner and outer health while competing and winning a trophy in a fitness competition two years later (you know the kind-the ones where they wear the itsy-bitsy-teeny-weeny-turquoise-rhinestone-string-bikinis). From losing my license to practice psychology and shutting down my practice to three years later, welcoming back nearly my entire clientele and now, being the owner of three successful businesses? That is the miracle of it all. It is the message of hope that I get to now share with others, so they know that there is recovery from pain—deep pain—and from addiction.

I grew up in Minnesota and enjoyed a wonderful childhood. It involved fun stuff like camping, softball, and playing in the neighborhood on hot summer days until the sun had set and your parents screamed your name to come inside. I was president of the church youth group and the choreographer for the high school dance team. I enjoyed straight As and was voted best-dressed my senior year. From the outside—I had it all—but if you had taken a good look at my insides, I was riddled with fear. It consumed me. The fear of not being good enough. The fear of being 'too much.' The fear of not fitting in. The fear that someday someone would discover I was a fraud.

Without knowing it at the time, I used perfectionism to hide my fears of unworthiness. I used it often, and I used it well. Perfectionism and I were buddies, or so I thought. Little did I know that perfectionism comes to steal and destroy, like the great accuser. It doesn't have your back, and it never had mine. It robs one of true authentic living, which then robs one of any chance at truly joyous living. However, I had no idea this is how it worked. I was clueless.

So I kept being perfect (wink, wink). I perfected it, you could say. I mastered it.

After high school, I was accepted into a prestigious, private, Christian college and again I excelled academically. I stayed in college earning advanced degrees for the next twelve years! I think I secretly knew this whole 'adult thing' was highly overrated and that I might not do so well at it. I met the love of my life, and we have been together ever since. However, when the school gig was up, and it was time to join the 'real world,' I was ill-equipped.

At the age of twenty-nine, we had our first daughter, Grace, and simultaneously it was time to get my first job and start building the career I had worked so hard for. My perfectionism had a field day! My daughter was my first true experience of perfectionism failing. Totally and completely. As you may be aware, it is impossible to be a perfect parent! My anxiety hit an all-time high. Was I failing? Should I be home with her? Did wanting a successful career mean I was selfish? When I was with her, I wanted to be working, and when I was working, I wanted to be with her. I wanted to be anywhere but inside of my skin. I could not escape myself. Still, up until this point, I was not drinking alcohol.

My pain had taken other forms before it showed up as the disease of alcoholism. I was addicted to people pleasing. I was addicted to high performance. I was addicted to outward measures of success. Anything to numb the pain of the intense fear of not being good enough. I like to call it my 'God-shaped hole' that I filled with everything *but* God. I tried filling the hole with food. I tried filling the hole with excessive exercise. I tried filling the hole with nice clothes, travel, and cars.

I landed my dream job at the university counseling center and thought I was finally on the right track to experiencing some happiness. Within months of starting, my male boss sexually harassed myself and two other female staff. After an arduous year of filing a complaint against him, we successfully made our case, and his tenure at the university was terminated. Unfortunately, we worked with staff members who didn't believe us, and they created a very hostile work environment. During the litigation, I took my state licensure exam to become a licensed psychologist. I failed the test because of my increasing depression, trauma, grief, and general anxiety. My greatest fear had come to fruition—I was indeed an imposter and a fraud, and now everyone knew it.

We became pregnant with our second daughter Emily. She was planned and we were so incredibly excited, but the C-section delivery was not planned and for a variety of reasons, I experienced it as extremely traumatic. I spiraled into a debilitating post-partum depression. I cried almost every day. The irritability and rage I would feel at times would overwhelm and frighten me. When she was one-year-old, I needed a reprieve. I decided to go to Minnesota for a week to my family's lake house with the intent to relax, be taken care of, lie on a raft all day, and allow my family to enjoy baby Emily and give me a much-needed break. Around 11 am on one of the first days of my visit, one of my family members brought me a vodka and cranberry. I had never drank hard alcohol except for an occasional margarita out with the girls. The feeling I experienced after that vodka and cranberry would forever change my life. For a moment, my depression lifted. For a moment, I was happy, and the committee in my head stopped talking and stopped accusing. I was carefree, and I loved it! I drank vodka and cranberry for the remainder of the week and took home with me what I believed to be an effective coping skill for my hectic, overwhelming life. Little did I know that what at first helped me disconnect from my depression would quickly disconnect me from my family, my values, my God, and myself.

Within one-year, I was a daily drinker. Within two years, I was a blackout drinker. Over the course of the next few years, I attempted to admit myself into a variety of substance abuse recovery programs and was repeatedly denied because I 'appeared' to have the perfect set up to be able to recover on an outpatient basis. I had a home. I had a job. I had a degree. I had a loving husband. What they didn't realize is I had all of those things, but did not have what I needed the most—recovery and an understanding of my disease. I thought I was bad trying to get good. I had no idea I was sick trying to get well—so I used my inability to get sober against myself and my shame reached astronomical levels. I concluded that if I had the most amazing husband and children and still couldn't stop drinking, then I really must be the most awful, selfish person. If I treated others who were mentally ill and couldn't help myself, then I must have serious characterological problems. If I couldn't do this for all of the reasons that I should, I must be the most ungrateful person alive.

After my time in jail, the judge ordered me to a thirty-day inpatient treatment program. I was ready. I had surrendered. I admitted to God and my innermost self that I was an alcoholic and was sick. That was the beginning of creating a life worth living. The perfectionism had to go. A new, authentic, real existence was being born. I recall entering treatment, and upon meeting my assigned counselor for the first time, she said, "Someday your children will benefit from what you are going to learn here." I remember thinking; *You must be smoking crack because no good could come from this.* I am happy to report she was right and I was wrong.

In those next thirty days, I learned how to join the human race. To sign up for all of it. The good, the bad, and the ugly. I started to take pride in being able to feel all of the emotions; even the ones that my perfectionism had told me were a sign of weakness for so long. I started redefining success, strength, and courage by taking risks and sharing the *real* me. The results were astounding. I began forming meaningful relationships that were close rather than surface-level. My vulnerability and truth seemed to give others permission to share *their* truth—*their* battle wounds and scars. I began to experience that the thing I feared the most-rejection-never happened and that the more I stepped into my true self, the closer people wanted to get to me.

Through a twelve-step program, I learned how to live. I learned the twelve-steps aren't a program to stop drinking—they are a program to start living. I took my inventory and learned to take ownership, to the best of my ability, for all of my feelings, expectations, and reactions to others. I made amends to those I wronged and started living a life of integrity. I fell in love with taking care of myself because I could see how doing so allowed me to show up for others. I went to the gym and started to practice the principles of the twelve-step program in all of my affairs, as I was taught. I cleaned house, so to speak. I stopped overspending and regained control over my finances. I stopped overeating and became spiritually fit as well as physically fit, and I did so seeking progress, not perfection.

My greatest fear is wasting my suffering and the suffering my loved ones experienced as a result of this disease. My intention, therefore, is to use what I have learned to inspire others, to give others hope, and show others that there is a spiritual solution to their physical malady. The power comes in the surrender. It comes when I say a simple three-step prayer: "God, I can't, you can, and I'm going to let you." I am happy to report I am a recovering perfectionist as well as a recovering alcoholic. Perfectionism nearly killed me, as did alcohol.

If I were to choose the 'superpower,' the 'mac-daddy' so to speak, of all of the tools that have helped me recover, hands down it would be gratitude. Gratitude and discontentment cannot hang out together. They are mutually exclusive. I like to say that my recovery program has successfully ruined my discontentment. I cannot stay discontent for long, and when I experience it, I have trained my brain to find something to be grateful for. Gratitude breeds happiness. It expands joy. It is a skill you can practice. Practice makes patterns. As a psychologist, I love knowing that by flexing the muscles of gratitude, so to speak, we can strengthen new pathways in our brain that become easy and natural over time.

It is safe to say the old me would not recognize the new me. The new me is the *true me*. The version of ourselves that we are all meant to be- the one who is worthy of an amazing, abundantly wonderful life. Bliss is our birthright. Anything other than that is just faulty learning-bad programming.

I have heard it said that shame cannot live when it is spoken of. I am not a walking bottle of alcohol. I am a human being who had experiences with alcohol because of experiences with pain. I am many beautiful things. I am a friend, mother, wife, teacher, therapist, healer, and child of God. I will not let alcohol define my worth. I will let it convict me to be the best version of myself that I can always be, striving for progress, not perfection.

Mohita Patel

Mohita is an integrative and functional medicine health coach. With her experience in the healthcare field and personal journey navigating chronic illness, she is passionate about educating, inspiring, and empowering people through their path with chronic health conditions.

In her coaching, she works one on one, runs group programs, and speaks locally to help people navigate their diagnosis using functional medicine principles and to take back their health, life and happiness.

She is a wife and mother of three amazing kids who are all an incredible support and part of this life's work!

Find Mohita online:

www.mohitapatel.com
www.facebook.com/mohitapatelcoaching/
mohita@mohitapatel.com

Chapter 19

Empowered to Heal

By Mohita Patel

When you're given a life-changing diagnosis, it arrives unannounced and completely takes over every part of your being. The diagnosis rips away all semblance of control. Suddenly, you're at its mercy as it dictates every decision you make, and every time you try to pull away, it just yanks you back to your harsh reality.

If I close my eyes for long enough, I can still remember the person I was before I was diagnosed with a chronic illness. I didn't know it then, but I was living with an abundance of blessings that I took for granted. I was in a great place with a career, home and family I loved deeply. I had no idea it could all crumble without warning. The memory of what life was like before feels like a vague dream lingering deep in my subconscious. The kind you wake up from and try desperately to remember the next day, but you fail knowing it's already long gone.

People with chronic disease often spend years in pain, feeling hopeless and exhausted, struggling to find someone who believes them and is willing to really listen. I was told I was one of the 'lucky few' who get diagnosed quickly.

When I began to notice the joint pain and fatigue, I brushed it off and carried on with life as usual. When my pain worsened, I stopped working my casual hours as a nurse and spent more time at home with my two young children. The pain and loss of mobility didn't improve, and within weeks of first noticing my symptoms, I was sitting in a rheumatologist's office.

"Your test results show you have rheumatoid arthritis," the doctor said.

I barely listened as he explained the life-long prognosis and all the life-threatening things that were going to happen to me if I didn't start medication right away (increased risk of heart disease, stroke and premature death by various causes).

He handed me some brochures and started talking about the medications I needed to take and the slew of side effects that came with them (an increased risk of cancer being one). I just stopped listening and a strange numbness set in. I wasn't used to being on the other side of a doctor's cold, detached statements. I was told to return in a week to discuss my treatment plan.

Once I was home, the thought of the diagnosis and treatment swirled around in my head. There were so many moments of numbness, falling apart, and crying. I was just thirty-four-years-old. How could all of this be happening to me? I had two small children. What was I supposed to do? How would I take care of them? Would I even be here for them? Why me?

Soon after my diagnosis, I ran into a neighbor. She shared that her mother had been diagnosed with rheumatoid arthritis and had fought the disease into remission with diet and lifestyle changes.

A small ray of hope shone, and I saw that there might be another way.

I took my husband to the follow-up appointment. At this point, I didn't know what I wanted to do, but I knew, in my gut, that taking drugs for the rest of my life wasn't the right answer for me. In the short-term, I had an out: my husband and I wanted a third child, and I couldn't get pregnant while on the medication. After we had told the doctor our pregnancy plans, we left his office and never looked back.

The rollercoaster of emotions that followed was difficult, volatile, and raw. It was easy to wallow in self-pity, anger, and bitterness. I wondered what I had done to bring this disease upon myself. Could I have lived healthier? Should I have done anything differently? It was so hard to feel positive or empowered and sure of my decisions when my body was falling apart.

I never knew what each day would bring and how it would affect me. Some days I couldn't move a couple of joints, others I couldn't even get myself out of bed. Whatever my daily struggle was, it came with extreme exhaustion, brain fog, and excruciating pain. Having to rely on someone to physically get through each day was profoundly demoralizing. On top of how it affected me physically, on an emotional level—it was destructive. I was broken. I had no will or energy to explore alternative options, but I continued to hear stories of others who had forgone conventional treatment and the ray of hope continued to glimmer, however faintly.

For months, I got progressively worse. My body was ravaged and exhausted. It was all I could do to get through one day at a time. I would look in the mirror and see someone I didn't even recognize. I was undernourished, weak, insecure, and struggling. I isolated myself because I figured, who would want to be around my pain and me? I felt I was never going to get better. In these times of overwhelm, it was hard not to wonder if I was making the right choices, or just destroying my life.

I had no clue what to do, or how to do it, but I needed to do something to improve my health. I figured I had hit my rock bottom and there was nowhere else to go but up. I had to leave the pity party, pick myself up and say, "No more!" I wasn't going to live in pain any longer.

A few months after my symptoms began; a blessing came my way in the form of pregnancy. It gave me a short reprieve from symptoms as my immune system calmed down. My body stopped attacking itself, and it was a time I could think again, become functional, and begin to piece together a path to healing.

I threw myself into finding out everything I could about alternative treatment options. I talked to everyone who could shed some light, and I poured over research. I was willing to learn and give anything a chance. I compiled information on nutrition, lifestyle changes, herbs, vitamins, supplements, yoga, acupuncture and anything else with a sliver of evidence. I had to figure out a path that made sense to me and felt right in my heart.

Every time I stalled in my journey, curiously the right connections always presented themselves. The synchronicity was so precise; it was hard to believe it was just coincidence. Sitting in a doctor's examination room, I stared at a screensaver with the word *Kaizen* floating endlessly across the monitor. It's a Japanese word that means change for the better. I kept asking myself, "How can I change? How can I make this better?"

After my son was born, life briefly felt normal again, until it didn't. There were days when I was in so much pain; I couldn't lift him or feed him. This time though, I was armed with my research and knew at least vaguely, what I needed to do to feel better. I changed my diet and paid attention to my sleep, stress, and exercise. These changes brought small improvements, and for the first time, I had hope about what was possible. Each step in the right direction gave me a deep sense of conviction and faith that things were going to be ok.

With everything I had gone through, I thought I knew what rock bottom was, but I was wrong.

My children developed chronic health issues. One daughter was in and out of the hospital and doctors' offices constantly. We were sent home with pain medications and no answers. To be sick yourself is one thing, but to watch your child and be utterly helpless is another. The guilt that I had let her down and couldn't help sent me into a tailspin, burying myself deeper and deeper in despair until I didn't know which way was up.

There is nothing I wouldn't have done to make her suffering and pain go away, to alleviate her struggle. To watch the strength of a child in adversity is humbling. I channeled every ounce of energy I had into healing and creating an environment where wellness would thrive. I knew I had to advocate and fight for what she needed.

It wasn't until I had to be strong for my kids that I prioritized *my* health. When I was doing it for myself, I would often derail myself and deal with the painful consequences. I have cried and wanted to give up more times than I can count. Even through every setback, it didn't matter as long as I was taking one-step after another no matter how small or slow, in the right direction.

I turned again to the research I'd put together when I was pregnant and committed myself to finding what would help my sick child and me. There was much trial and error, struggle and frustration, but slowly I figured out a plan based on functional medicine principles that worked for us. The most significant change was in how we approached food. We focus so much on eating for pleasure; we forget that every bite fuels and nourishes us. Food can be a powerful healer when we choose to take in what our body needs to thrive. I knew everything I put in my mouth was either helping or hurting and I was eating to heal. I continued to focus on self-care and harnessing the power of the mind to bring healing. I didn't have every answer yet, but I knew I was on the right path.

It's easy to fall into the trap of becoming your diagnosis. The language of conventional medicine is steeped in negativity. A disease is 'failure,' a 'betrayal by your body,' or your body 'attacking you.' This narrative all too quickly becomes our story, and we let it define us and how we live.

It's hard to detach from the messaging and make self-guided decisions. It takes a lot of courage to stand up and say "No! This is not what my life will be," to forgive your body for the perceived betrayal and to love yourself unconditionally (diagnosis and all) as an integral part of who you are.

It wasn't until I began to accept and love myself unconditionally and put myself first that I saw significant changes in my health. Progress was slow, but slow progress was still progress. In time, I regained my health, life, and happiness. I haven't used medication in six years, and I am symptom-free. There are no quick fixes, and no one said the road would be easy, but it is worth it.

Along the way, I met an amazing community of like-minded people all supporting each other on journeys through chronic illness. In time, I put together an incredible team of integrative doctors, acupuncturists, chiropractors, massage therapists, family, and friends. Each new change I implemented took my kids and me closer to healing physically and emotionally. Every inch forward brought the light at the end of the tunnel closer.

As my physical health changed, I also had an enormous shift in my mindset. I made a conscious choice to focus on my ideal state and chose to live looking forward and never back. I learned to reframe everything. The changes I made, like my restrictive diet and regimented lifestyle choices, weren't losses, sacrifices, or deprivation. When I saw them as choices that brought me health and happiness, life became infinitely easier.

Alongside this, I needed to have faith and believe that being well was possible for me. I couldn't let all my fear and doubt consume me. I had to be loving, forgiving and patient with myself. Real change only happened when I wanted it more than anything else. There is no one on this planet that could have done what I needed to do for me.

Being chronically sick forced me to discern and prioritize what I value. I deliberately created space for that which uplifted me while steering clear of that which brought me down. I learned early on that there are people who will stand by you through hardship, and there are others who will leave you in your darkest and weakest moments. An important part of healing for me was having the grace to let those people go because they held me back from finding peace and healing.

I used to feel resentful and longed for times when my life was easier. However, the more time passes, I settle into a state of gratitude and acceptance for what it allowed me to grow into.

It is possible to rise from the ashes. Know that there is always enough abundance and guidance from the Universe. It surrounds us, and each of us has the power to change our story. We are not chained to the past. Happiness doesn't just happen to us. Our trials are an opportunity to find ourselves, evolve and grow, because we are stronger than we could ever believe possible. We create our destiny and each day we may stumble, but we grow, we learn, and we get better, and better still. We just have to continue to show up for our self, one moment at a time and we will always be able to take on whatever comes our way.

Today, my passion is helping people with chronic conditions. I hope to educate, inspire, and empower others through their own journey. I'm incredibly grateful for the opportunity to now guide others who struggle and want to lift themselves out of their darkness.

I believe so strongly in the body's innate ability to overcome chronic disease and heal when given what it needs to thrive. We're led to believe life-long treatment with drugs is the only option, but my own experience and that of others prove otherwise. These miracles that defy conventional medicine are not miraculous. They're simply people with the determination to ask the right questions, challenge norms and seek answers.

Taking my life back from a chronic illness is the hardest thing I have ever done, but what keeps me going is knowing how far I have come. Life isn't perfect, and there will always be challenges, but facing these challenges is worth it.

I may have lost the person I once was, but I don't for a minute regret the person I have become or the journey that it took me on.

I have a condition that will never truly go away. I will always have it, but I live with empowerment, knowing that I am in control and I dictate how my chapter will be written and how my story unfolds.

Awilda Rivera Prignano

Awilda was born and raised in Chicago, IL in a bi-lingual/bi-cultural home and is fluent in Spanish. Writing has been her constant passion but she also loves traveling, interior design and pampering herself when she can.

Awilda has an extensive career in sales and retail management spanning over thirty years. She is currently a transformational coach who helps individuals become the best version of themselves through lasting habit change and self-care. Awilda has been through it all. She knows first-hand that change is possible when you put your heart and mind into it.

Awilda is also a Happy Giver on Happy, an app that connects people going through life's everyday struggles with exceptionally compassionate listeners.

Find Awilda online:

awildathehealthcoach@gmail.com

Chapter 20

The Thriving Monkey

By Awilda Rivera Prignano

My story will start another day. In fact, my whole life was scheduled for 'another day.' That's when I would take time off work, relax and have fun for once.

I like to think I'm a bit like a cheeky monkey: happy, free, and thriving. However, for most of my life, all I could think of was work. I'm a workaholic.

It took hitting rock bottom financially and physically five years ago for me to wake up. There's no such day as 'another day.' There's right now, or there's never.

Right now, I'm fresh out of a yearly review in a job I love. My boss was reviewing my financials and told me my potential for one-year from now. He gave me a number that was almost unbelievable considering five years ago I barely had $20 to my name.

It might be helpful to know how I became a workaholic. My mother and father worked immensely hard. I remember Mom taking care of my siblings and me in the morning, then going to work with my dad at the family store all day, before she came home to make us dinner and put us to bed. She often waited until Dad was home to eat dinner with him, most nights as late as 10 pm. Hard work was the rule, not the exception.

As a freshman in college, I started working, and it became part of my identity. It gives me validation and power. It keeps me young and makes me feel alive. I thrive on it. Or, I thought I did, but a woman can't survive on work alone.

A psychic reading changed everything for me. I try to get a psychic reading at least once a year. Maybe I read too much into it, but I love it. At this reading, my psychic told me some painful things about how I was missing out on life, and how fun seemed to be non-existent for me.

Then he said something that I really listened to. He mentioned work. "You will start a new job; you will experience many changes. You will have a new adventure," he said. "The number eleven will make a profound difference in your life," he added.

He was as vague as you'd expect a psychic to be. I didn't know if eleven meant 2011, eleven months from now, the eleventh month or something else. All he said was the number eleven would be significant.

I left my reading confident in only one thing: change was coming. It seemed like a good thing. Life had been the same for a long time: work, be a good mom, work more, allow myself a few indulgences with the usual guilt, and work some more. It wasn't perfect, but it was my normal.

I was less confident about the job issue he mentioned. I was only a year into a job I enjoyed, and while it wasn't going to be the place I retired from, I planned to stick around for a few years.

It wasn't long after my reading that I got a call from a former colleague. His employer was looking to hire an experienced retail manager. My first thought was, *This might be the new job my psychic mentioned.* My second thought was, *Why not? I have nothing to lose.*

The interview was booked for April 2nd, an auspicious date. It was my late husband's birthday. I'd been widowed young and ever since I've felt that my husband was always watching over our daughter and me, protecting us. It was a good sign.

I approached my interview with confidence, open to whatever the opportunity turned out to be. It went very well, but I heard nothing in the weeks that followed. I got in touch with the friend who had referred me and asked what was up. It turned out, the district manager had just welcomed a new baby into his family and wasn't able to follow-up with me. He assumed I would have lost interest. I made it clear I was open to an offer if there was one coming. When he called me, the offer was too good to pass up. It was significantly greater than my current salary, with a signing incentive and an excellent benefits package. It was a no-brainer.

With better benefits, I felt it was time to get checked by a doctor. I hadn't been feeling well, and a friend had told me about a great program through a doctor's office to get me on track to losing weight and getting healthy.

The initial testing—a questionnaire and urine analysis—went fine. Then the blood work. What a nightmare. I always have problems giving blood because my veins are freakishly small. I warned the phlebotomist. For an hour, she tried everything she could think of to tap my veins. Nothing worked. The phlebotomist was so kind and patient as she turned to one last option. She fetched some heating pads that are used to keep newborns warm. After she laid them over my hand for a while, she could finally draw enough for the tests.

Someone probably should have seen it as a sign. Something was very wrong.

When I came back a month later for my results, the practitioner was shocked to see me standing in front of her. "I can't explain how you're even able to function! How did you even drive here?" she said. She told me to go straight to the emergency room. Apparently, my red blood cell count was abnormally low due to a severe iron deficiency, and I was also dehydrated.

I drove myself to the hospital, suddenly realizing how hungry I was. I hadn't eaten that morning in case I needed more tests. I stopped to get an omelet, my favorite meal. Who knew what was in store for me or when I would eat a normal meal again?

The health professionals at the hospital saw the same thing as the doctor's office. I was checked in immediately, and they told me I was severely anemic. I had no idea. I knew I was tuckered out, but that just came along with working a lot, right?

It was a little more than that. I ignored my body's cry for help. I took the paleness of my face, the occasional dizzy spells, and the chronic fatigue as normal. I updated my boss on my status as soon as I could. Work is *that* important to me. It was constantly on my mind.

While they were prepping me for the first blood transfusion, I called my daughter. To my surprise, she came straight to the hospital. It was a surprise because I had always felt there was some resentment from her over how much I worked and now I was in the hospital because of it.

When she was young, close family, friends, or daycare workers (when I could afford it) always cared for her. The night before, we'd had dinner together, and she told me she had just been at a wake for a close friend's father. I think it was her first time experiencing death. She was only thirteen-months-old when her father died. Seeing her rush to the hospital gave me comfort I had no idea I was missing.

I was back to work shortly after my stint in the hospital, but I took some time off a few weeks later to go to Las Vegas with my daughter. It was a belated treat for her 21st birthday as we hadn't spent time together (just the two of us) in ages. We had so much fun! I encouraged her to pick where we went and what we did. It ended up being a lot of walking, and I started to feel severe pain in my lower back. I didn't mention it for fear it would disrupt our fun.

I was back to work. It was Labor Day, which meant long lines and crowds everywhere. My back was still hurting, but I'd just started this job and had already been in the hospital once. I didn't want to get a reputation for being the girl who's always sick. I made it through my shift and booked a massage for that evening. It didn't help, so I went home and took some painkillers to help me fall asleep.

The next morning, I was too sore to get out of bed. I phoned my assistant at work and explained how I was feeling. "Go to the emergency room," she said. "We have insurance, and this is what it's for."

I gathered the strength to drive myself to the hospital. Again, the staff were shocked to see me standing. I learned I not only had kidney stones but a severe infection in my left kidney.

If I hadn't driven myself to the hospital that day, I might have died. I wouldn't have even been in the hospital if my assistant hadn't urged me to go. I was trapped in a cycle of not valuing myself enough to get the help I needed. I didn't even know myself well enough to realize when my life was threatened. It was hard to admit that. I didn't know how to fix it, so I did what I always do, I went back to work.

There was another hospital visit in my future. I'd been seeing my gynecologist because cysts were growing on my uterus. That was causing the iron deficiency, and in turn, the anemia. I decided to get a hysterectomy.

This time, I was booking a procedure ahead of time. I also took a leave of absence from work to recover. My eyes were wide open and I knew I needed to change my habits or this cycle of health-related drama would never end. I had put myself last on my priority list for too long.

My surgery would be in early December after my kidney infection was fully treated and my stones removed. My daughter drove me to the hospital and stayed there throughout the surgery. When I woke up, I had an unusual feeling. I felt like I had just delivered a baby, yet there was no baby. There would never be another baby. Even though I was probably too old for pregnancy, the loss I felt was unexpected.

On a sunny Friday morning, a week after my surgery, I woke up with another unfamiliar feeling. I felt refreshed, happy. After so many months of pain, I was free! I made myself an omelet, to celebrate! Then I got a call from a friend at work. Our branch of our parent company was closing. I was shocked, but not devastated. *I've survived a layoff before*, I thought, *and I've endured months of trauma and pain. I can get through this.*

I took a generous severance package, and for the first time since I was a teenager, I enjoyed the holiday season without the crush of working retail. For so many years, Christmas was just a day off to recover from being overworked. Now I was able to embrace the season. I sent out Christmas cards and made time to catch up with family and friends.

It became clear to me that I'd spent a long time shrugging off all the parties I'd missed and friends I'd lost touch with. I had made excuses that there would be another party, another time, another day. Not this time. This time would be different.

I took time for *me* in the months that followed. I didn't rush to get back to work. I went to the library every day and read books (something I was always too tired to do previously). I caught up on TV shows and movies I'd missed. I traveled to new places, met new people, and reconnected with old friends. I went to summer festivals, tried different kinds of foods, and learned to cook.

When I started to see the number eleven everywhere, I knew I was on the right path. I was finally following my intuition and making the changes I needed to grow. I was learning about myself, to love myself and to give myself the attention I deserved.

Once I had healed my body and soul, I was ready to look for work. I thought it would come as easy as it had in the past. My resume was strong, and I had confidence in my abilities.

I sent out resume after resume, attended workshops and did many interviews, but nothing came of it. The country was in a deep recession. Eventually, my employment insurance ran out. I put everything I owned into storage and moved in with my mother. She'd been ill and had wanted me to move in for a while. With my savings drained, I had no reason not to.

I remember sitting in my mom's living room in the dark one night wondering, *How did I get here?* I knew my pride was holding me back. I worked so hard in my career to be at a particular pay status; it felt insulting to be offered less. It was as if these companies could smell the desperation and wanted to take advantage.

I cried it out, splashed water on my face and turned to my computer. I knew that if I dug deep, I would find an answer.

I sifted through my connections, and their connections, for someone I hadn't reached out to yet. Boom. I found a couple of leads and emailed them. The next day, one of those connections emailed me and asked if I was looking for work. Yes! After a few more interviews, I was working again! It was in a different field, in sales instead of retail. I was grateful for the opportunity to be getting a paycheck again. The money was significantly less than what I was used to, but I learned to make it work. After all, I was meant to be there.

That job led me to the boss who just did my yearly review, which brings me back to the start of my story. After he had told me my earning potential, I told him how truly blessed I felt. He nodded in agreement, though he didn't know the journey it took. I am proud of the tenacity and confidence I was able to demonstrate to get me here.

You might call me a recovering workaholic now. I love what I do, and sometimes I still work long hours, but I do that on my own terms. I leave work at work. I value my personal time and my good health. I'm happy, and I'm thriving.

When my boss initially interviewed me for this position, he asked me one of those silly interview questions that people usually brush off: "If you were an animal, which animal would you be?"

"A monkey!" I said, without hesitation.

"Why?" he asked, probably expecting a predator or a workhorse.

"Monkeys are smart, boundlessly happy, and they know how to thrive."

Allison Tuffs

Allison is a wife, mother, nutritionist, lifestyle educator, writer, and entrepreneur. These are labels society gives her, but who is she?

Allison is the woman that had it all, or so she thought until the Universe gave her the cosmic kick in the pants, not once, but twice. Life experiences forced her down a path of choice, choices that led to a complete happiness over-haul. Allison is a choice empowerment coach that helps women lean into hidden feelings and emotions, move into health and build an energized life they are happy to live, not for the label, but because it brings them joy.

Find Allison online:

www.AllisonTuffs.com
https://www.facebook.com/UpYourEnergy/

Chapter 21

Fatigue - The Stealer of Life

By Allison Tuffs

I remember when I was a child. I had so much energy and found so much joy in the minutest of details. I recall running across the grass, my blond curly hair flowing, blue eyes sparkling, all just to see a bug that my brother and sister had caught. It was so exciting.

Everything was exciting. Life was one big ball of adventure and new experiences. I had the energy of the Ever Ready bunny. I'd go and go until I hit a wall and sleep would take me. Sleep was blissful, peaceful, and above all—rejuvenating. I was so excited about life my mom would have to remind me to eat and go to the toilet.

Those days were filled with joy. As I went through life, that energy remained, and I became passionate about learning and challenges.

As a standard type-A personality, I thrived on new. New experiences, new adventures, and new challenges were my jam. I was ambitious, athletic, striving, learning, and growing.

Life ticked along, and I was very successful. I worked around the world with humanitarian organizations and with the United Nations. I had three beautiful children and did an MBA while I was working full-time and raising three small babies. I had energy to burn. In my forties, I was *still* like the Ever Ready bunny.

Then things changed. I started to fatigue; I began to get snappy, forgetful and irritable with my kids. Then to our surprise, I became pregnant with our fourth child, and I was launched from tired into debilitating exhaustion, and I mean *debilitating*. I would lie on the floor in my office at lunch and sleep. It was early to bed and late to rise with naps wherever I could grab them. This became my life.

After the birth, I recovered my energy slightly but having a newborn with three kids in tow is a tiring experience. I put my exhaustion down to being a new mom, even though I'd never experienced this with the other three births. This was different, but I was busy, so I ignored the warning signs and carried on.

Then the unimaginable happened, my beautiful baby girl, Kataryna, died just before her fifth month of life. Shock, disbelief and an inability to process the loss saw me return to work within two weeks of her passing. I threw myself into work, raised my three youngsters and did my level best to pretend life was ok. I became a robot. Life was on autopilot. To others, things looked normal but internally I couldn't shake the low energy. I explained it away and marched on like a good soldier.

Months later, my body rebelled, and I found myself in the Beirut hospital having a myriad of tests done. I was diagnosed with Hashimoto's, an autoimmune thyroid disease. From the moment of my diagnosis, I set about trying to get off the life-long thyroid meds.

Enter yoga and meditation, two of the best things that happened in my life. I loved Saturday mornings because even though I was completely exhausted, I was able to carve out space on the mat where I could breathe and move through the pain that wracked my spirit. After the yoga practice, I'd crawl back into bed and sleep until noon when my husband couldn't keep the kids out any longer. They'd jump on the bed saying, "Mommy, Mommy get up," and I would, but I longed for the bed.

Those days were tough, but yoga made it easier, and my husband was a godsend.

Fast forward a few years. The exhaustion remained and was compounded by migraines and terrible stomach problems. Food was becoming an enemy and Imodium was my best friend. I lost sight of myself and had become a new person enveloped in the grief, exhaustion, and fear of how my body would respond to anything I put in my mouth.

I didn't understand what was happening to me. As a nutritionist and healthcare professional, I'd always taken good care of my family and myself. We ate well, juiced, made our own bread, added additional fiber to meals and snacks, and cut out processed foods. Nothing helped. This frustrated me and made me feel incompetent. I was doing everything right, but I wasn't coming back to my old self.

After years of exhaustion, the debilitating joint pain started. I couldn't open a jar or cut an apple. The digression was slow and ruthless. The pain was constant, and it robbed me of my life. The ability to care for my kids, to make a meal, do yoga, and perform at work on a computer were taken away. Trips to Beirut for doctor's appointments, popping prescription painkillers and anti-inflammatory medications became a way of life.

Life wasn't fun, yet watching my kids' energy and enthusiasm for life kept me dreaming and longing for a return to my former self. Above all, I wanted their energy and happiness. Thankfully kids have a way of making everyone happy, so I had laughter and joy in my life, but energy and health were what I craved.

I was fed up, and I wanted my life back. I knew if I wanted to feel more energized it had to come from within, and it would require making difficult lifestyle choices. With both feet, I jumped into the puddle of stagnant water that had become my life and went to work on getting in touch with how I nourished my mind and body.

Being on sick leave gives one a lot of time. Time to have long leisurely soaks in the bathtub and read—a lot. While the kids were at school, I spent my time soaking and reading personal development and self-awareness books. As I read, I asked myself questions and slowly the steel trap door that had slammed shut when Kateryna passed away—opened a crack—and light started to replace the darkness.

During those long healing baths, I started to let the pain in my heart bubble up and in the sanctity of the bathroom; I made a choice to let it out. It was there, in the tub that a glimmer of a new life and a new career started to form.

Even though I had a strong food background with a Bachelor and Master of Science in Nutrition, it had been years since I graduated and my intuition was gnawing at me to delve into the alternative healthcare world. After all, I'd tried the conventional way: healthy eating, doctors and medication and nothing alleviated the fatigue, irritability, pain and constant stomach upset. I had nothing to lose.

The decision to take on more study wasn't easy. I was having a hard time focusing and remembering things. I had no idea how I would ever be able to retain what I learned, but I jumped, followed my heart, and enrolled in a holistic nutrition course.

It was the best thing I ever did. It opened my whole world, and it challenged the beliefs I had acquired going through the dietetics program at university. I was like a wide-eyed kid! The learning fascinated my mind, and I became a knowledge sponge.

Our home and kitchen began to change. Adaptogenic herbs appeared, and I tossed the prescription anti-inflammatories. They weren't working anyway, the pain was always there, and I was learning how they damage the intestinal track where 70% of a person's immunity resides. I had an autoimmune disease, so I put two and two together and decided I was doing more harm than good.

Pills were replaced with food, herbs, and an incredible chiropractor. In those first few sessions, he adjusted my body, but it released something deep within me and floods of emotion came out. I remember one time my daughter was with me, and after an adjustment, the tears welled up and flowed. She thought he had hurt me; he hadn't. It was a just a deep emotional release.

Miraculously, the pain in my arms started to dissipate, and I could wield a knife again, which made meal prep easier. Slowly my energy levels improved, and I could play with the kids and work on a computer. Yippee!

I returned to work. The hours sitting at a computer were managed by wearing wrist splints, and while my energy levels had improved enough to survive the days, I was tapped out for anything more. I'd return home drained and then flake on the couch. Never mind playing with the kids, ha, I barely had the energy to *watch* them play. Instead of me tucking them into bed, they were tucking me in, and they were under ten-years-old.

This wasn't right. This was no way to live. There had to be more than this in my future. I couldn't believe that this was a natural part of aging. I had a hard time buying that aches, pains, fatigue, and memory loss were just par for the course. How could it be, it didn't make sense. Obsessed with having some of the kids' energy and encouraged by the success I'd had in at least getting well enough to get back to work, I kept exploring, and my energy kept elevating.

On this self-discovery path in January 2014, my brother and I attended a weeklong workshop in London. I returned to Lebanon riding high on life, with a vision to continue expanding my energy and knowledge and help others to get their life back too. There was no doubt I was on the right path; I was fired up.

That night I went to bed on top of the world. I had a plan, a direction, and goals. Then I woke up in the middle of the night, and for a brief moment, something was off. I couldn't swallow. In the coming days, my life did a complete summersault, and I was diagnosed with a carotid artery and brain aneurysm and scheduled for surgery.

I went from fired up with direction to lost and confused—again.

In preparation for the surgery, I had to get clearance from my endocrinologist, cardiologist, neurologist, rheumatologist and a vascular surgeon. To each, I asked one question: "Could this be diet related." Unequivocally they all said no. In medical speak, no means the literature doesn't support that theory, or it's not been documented, so no.

With surgery behind me, we waited for the tissue analysis to determine the mysterious cause of all these challenges I'd been experiencing. The results were negative for every known genetic disease. I was relieved, but I was also left asking why? What's the root cause?

I refused to believe this was normal. In what kind of hell was this normal? I vowed that this would not be my life. I resigned from work leaving a sixteen-year career with the United Nations and dedicated my life and energy to getting well so I could be with my kids and not just watch them grow up. I wanted an active part in their lives.

On the path to health, there was one stone I'd left unturned, one that I refused to engage because it was hard, uncomfortable and scary. It was the path of doing a complete elimination diet. I'd read Terry Wahl's book, *The Wahl's Protocol*. She had gotten her life back with diet changes, and I thought, *If she can, so can I.*

Again, I jumped and embraced a thirty-day elimination diet. As a nutritionist and student of holistic health, I knew how to do it, but I didn't want to believe my precious food was the root of my problems.

By day four I was covered in hives and taking medication to manage the attack, so much for no pills. By day seven the hives subsided, and the pills were tossed. By day fifteen, I was shocked at how amazing I felt. The pain was all but gone, my head shaking was lessening, I was sleeping, and my toilet trips became normal. By day thirty, I had my life back and was tickled pink.

I traveled to Canada shortly after this to visit my parents. We went to the Keg, my favorite restaurant, and had a teriyaki steak dinner. Within twenty-four hours, my world crashed down around me. My hands and feet tingled; I lived in the toilet, and my energy was depleted. I could barely get up off the couch to visit friends. That's when I knew. This was diet related; it had all been diet related.

Back in Lebanon, I had three tests for celiac disease and tests for parasites. All were positive. Unbelievable! The fix was easy, or so my education led me to believe. Avoiding gluten for life is the prescription, but it's not so easy in reality. My upbringing and whole culture evolved around gluten containing foods. Switching gluten free for gluten is no substitute. I tried it though; the food tasted gross, but something else was at play.

I felt terrible, again. I was eating gluten free cookies, bread, etc. but felt awful. Not at all like I felt on the elimination diet. There was something else I was eating that was killing my energy. Back to the drawing board.

A blood IgG food sensitivity panel answered my remaining questions. Millet and a range of other foods were off the chart for me, meaning they too would have to be removed for me to recapture health.

Today, years down the track, my learning has continued, and my energy and health have responded exponentially. I've found my perfect balance of diet and lifestyle that energizes me and nourishes my being. I've retrained as a fitness instructor so I can share my experience with others who are slashing their way through the jungle of poor health, grief, and disbelief. I support and coach them so they can find their perfect balance and reclaim their energy and life.

A deep visceral longing for quality of life drove my lifestyle and career changes. In summary, the lessons learned on this journey came down to learning how to trust in myself, and in my body to heal itself. The hardest choices I faced and continue to face are within myself. I ask and answer internal questions daily about what I want versus what I need.

I am free. I have my life, health, and energy back because of lifestyle choices that are right for me. Not easy, but *right*. I am grateful for the strength and the ability to choose. It's possible for you too.

Kelli Verbosh

After a life-changing surgery, Kelli found herself at a crossroads when she tried to get back to a normal life. For years, she felt stuck and uninspired. Kelli loved raising her young daughters, but there was a fire kindling inside, hinting that she was capable of something more. It led her on a path of self-improvement: body, mind and spirit.

Kelli found passion in sharing her journey with others and raising them to new heights in their physical and financial health through her business coaching. Her organization has impacted thousands and she's proven that authenticity attracts the right people. Kelli has a following of over three thousand people on social media and she's proud to be a director on the board for the Get Well Gabby Foundation.

Find Kelli online:

www.kelliverbosh.com
Kelli@kelliverbosh.com
www.getwellgabby.org
http://www.facebook.com/thrivewithpurpose

Chapter 22

The Road from Brain Surgery is Paved with Potholes

By Kelli Verbosh

"You have a mass in your head." I'll never forget the day I heard those words through the phone. I sat at my desk surrounded by co-workers, sobbing. I was sent home, and I could barely see through my tears on my thirty-minute commute.

I'd prepared myself for many things when I started talking to my OB/GYN about my struggles with my husband to get pregnant. A tumor was not one of those things. My doctor had ordered an MRI "Just in case," before she referred me to a fertility specialist. It was just to "Rule things out."

My husband Kevin and I went to see a neurosurgeon. He said the tumor had to come out as soon as possible or I'd risk blindness. My diagnosis was a low-grade astrocytoma coming from the hypothalamus. Brain cancer. "Low-grade" doesn't sound so bad, and it wasn't terminal, but because of the location, I needed a craniotomy. That's when they drill into your skull, remove some bone and do brain surgery. It's risky. Putting your trust in someone whose hands are going to be inside your brain is not an easy thing.

Kevin and I spent many nights lying in bed crying. He was devastated. He had lost his mom to breast cancer when he was a boy. The trauma from his childhood came flooding back, and he was terrified at the thought that I might not make it. I felt responsible for his pain. I felt like I had ruined his life but I tried to be strong for us both.

As I prepped for brain surgery two months after my diagnosis, I thought about my parents. I was their only child. What if I didn't come out of surgery? I signed papers acknowledging my death was a possibility.

The day of my surgery, I was surrounded by my husband, parents, my in-laws, my godparents, and two cousins who were like sisters to me. I said goodbye in tears, unsure if I would see them again. The last thing I remember as the general anesthetic took hold was the surgical team making small talk as they wheeled me away.

Later that day, I woke up in ICU. The surgery went fine, but I had no idea of the long road to recovery ahead. After a day or two, my occupational therapist had me up and taking slow walks. When I was discharged, I lay in the backseat of our car feeling pain wrack my head every time we hit a bump in the road, which seemed to be made entirely of potholes.

My parents moved in with us for my expected month-long recovery period to help care for me. I had little strength. I was thirty-three-years-old, and I had to be bathed. My mom brushed my hair for me. I couldn't believe this was my life. I had wanted to come home from a hospital with a baby, not three titanium screws holding my skull together.

I was watching a movie at home three days after discharge when I suffered a grand mal seizure. I had to be helicoptered to the nearest trauma center for immediate care. It turns out we hadn't been monitoring my electrolytes properly. All I remember is when I eventually woke up in the hospital, I was painfully thirsty but nobody would let me drink anything because I apparently had edema and was filled with water.

In the weeks following, I made daily progress in my recovery. However, some strange side effects began. Things nobody warned me about before surgery when my concern was simply surviving. I was constantly urinating because the trauma of brain surgery gave me a deficiency in the hormone that controls urine output. Imagine having to pee every ten minutes and being so desperately thirsty that all you can think about is water and fruit.

On top of that fun, I began to gain weight rapidly and uncontrollably. I was gaining several pounds each week, and there was seemingly nothing I could do. I grew from a size six to a size twelve in about three months. It didn't make any sense. I'd always been in control of my weight and worked hard to keep healthy habits. My doctors had no explanation either and didn't seem to acknowledge a concern at my follow-up visits, making it all the more frustrating.

I was back to work a couple of months after my surgery, but my seizure meant I wasn't allowed to drive for six months. My parents were amazing, staying longer than originally planned and helping me get to and from work so life could be a little bit normal.

I kept gaining, grasping for a bit of control over the drastic weight gain. Eventually, when I fully recovered from the surgery, I joined a gym, hired a personal trainer and sweated hard. However, seven months later, I had gained another twenty-five pounds—

and I'm not talking about muscle. I would gain, stabilize for a while, and gain again. I had never felt so powerless.

About six months after my surgery, I was cleared to start fertility treatments. I tried to let go of the frustration I felt over my weight and just focus on growing our family. Finally, I felt like I could get back on track with my life plan.

Our second round of fertility treatment was successful, and I was pregnant! As if that wasn't enough excitement, we were expecting twins! After so much struggle, I felt doubly blessed. Kevin and I started planning a life with our little boy and girl, dreaming contentedly of our perfect family.

Twenty-nine weeks into my pregnancy, we lost our little boy. His heart stopped beating, and we don't know why. We will never know why.

A few weeks later, I delivered a beautiful, healthy little girl. Kevin and I cried tears of joy when we heard her first screams. We named her after Kevin's mom. Her brother, Jack, followed. The swirl of conflicting emotions was indescribable. We had a little girl to welcome into the world. We were able to hold our son and say goodbye. We laid him to rest with his grandmother, and we know he remains our angel, protecting us all.

I wondered if I was being punished. We all do things in life that we aren't proud of. I thought that I was being punished for those things. A brain tumor. A damaged metabolism that wreaked havoc on my body and demolished my self-confidence. A child I had to deliver stillborn. Was there a lesson in it all or was I just destined to have bad things happen to me? I was desperate to find meaning in it all. All that pain had to exist for a reason—didn't it?

Our daughter was four when Kevin and I tried fertility treatments again. I miscarried the day I was leaving for a weekend event out of town. It was extremely distressing, and I couldn't help feeling responsible. Part of me remained optimistic that we would have a successful pregnancy one day, though partly I couldn't help wondering, "Why me?"

However, there was so much joy yet to come. I became pregnant again, and that time, I took the pregnancy extremely seriously. I stuck to every precaution they give you about being pregnant and was exceptionally cautious about anything that might be a risk to the pregnancy. When our daughter was five, I welcomed a healthy set of twins into the world. This time, two beautiful girls that I was able to keep alive. Our three girls have brought such happiness into our lives, but a day doesn't go by that I don't think about our little boy, Jack, and wish he was with us.

While I had so many reasons to feel blessed, I continued to suffer the effects of a damaged metabolism. After years of consultation, doctors deduced I had irreversible damage to the hypothalamus area of my brain where thirst and hunger are controlled. Whether I eat a healthy salad or a sugary cookie, I will metabolize it the same way. It's a rare condition experienced by a small percentage of people with similar types of tumors. There is no known treatment or cure.

I refused to accept this lack of control and made it my quest to find answers. I spent a ton of money on trainers, nutritionists, gyms, fad diets and weight-loss centers with no results. So I kept searching and searching.

Meanwhile, I was raising my young daughters and couldn't help feeling stuck in life. I knew I was capable of doing more than laundry and dishes.

I knew I didn't want to go back to the last career I'd had. When my eldest was a year old, I was laid off. I went back to school at that time to become an MRI technologist because I was inspired by the tech who had once shown me so much grace and humanity. However, when I began work as an imaging technologist, I didn't like it at all. It didn't feel like me. Soon after the twins turned two, I took the opportunity to make a change.

As a mother of three, I realized I could choose to be satisfied with having lived through those tough years, or I could decide to keep growing and find meaning in it all. I wanted to show my daughters that moms could be at home and still have a career of their choosing. I wanted to make the most of the life I had.

I eventually found a solution for both my health and my motivation in a product a friend of mine was selling. I was skeptical, but it had a thirty-day money back guarantee, and nothing else had worked, so I tried it. I started nurturing my body with high doses of nutrients, minerals, and vitamins. To my surprise, the weight started falling off immediately. I lost more weight in a week than I had in years of trying other solutions.

I lost enough weight to regain some confidence, relieve pressure on my joints, help me feel more comfortable in my clothes, and allow me to move around better. Most importantly, I'd proved so many of my doctors wrong. They had said my condition meant I would never be able to lose weight. Now, I had shocked my metabolism with so much goodness that it actually reacted.

Beyond my weight-loss, I saw improvements in my mood and my sleep, and I had more patience with my kids. It all combined to help me show up in life as a better mom and a better wife. It was an immense relief, and I felt better than I had in years.

It wasn't a miracle product—I still had some weight-loss ahead of me, but I was elated at the progress. If this product worked for my rare metabolic disorder, imagine what it could do for other women. I began sharing the product, first to friends and family who noticed the changes in me and then to a wider network. By accident, I found out I was really good at this entrepreneurship thing.

I began to see the network marketing business as a vehicle for me to help other people. I felt empowered in a way I hadn't since before my tumor, and I wanted to spread the feeling. I'd figured it out; this was the reason I had to go through everything. This was the path that God had intended for me. I was here to help people find clarity, energy, and focus and it filled me with purpose.

My drive became, "How many lives can I impact? Can I help people achieve a life change?" I had found a career with a purpose that allowed me to tell a story. A story I used to think was unfair and made me bitter was now an opportunity for personal growth.

I soon realized there were other stay at home moms—and working moms too—who felt stuck and frustrated like I had. We were all told to go to school, get a job and work the rest of our lives until we retired with very little money to live on. Most people spend their life in debt, living for the weekends to spend precious time with their family. Are they living or just existing?

I had taken the kind of journey that allowed me to help others and I was going to tell everyone about it. I've been able to support people through physical, psychological and even financial transformations. This isn't a hobby; it's a legacy business that someday my daughters can be part of.

It has been almost eleven years since my brain surgery. From the start, under all the stress and fear, I always knew how fortunate I was that I didn't have terminal brain cancer. After surgery, I looked for ways to help in the cancer community, and I am honored to be partnered with a local non-profit called the Get Well Gabby Foundation. Gabby was five when she fought a three-and-a-half month battle with an aggressive brain tumor. Her short life ended right before her sixth birthday. I help raise funds for their mission of helping local families dealing with a childhood cancer diagnosis as well as lifting the spirits of the little warriors fighting for their lives in local oncology units. It's my way of showing gratitude that I'm still here while too many children die too young.

I still struggle at times because on the outside; I am not the perfect picture of health. But I know my metabolism doesn't define me. Health comes in all shapes and sizes, and I help people get healthy on the inside first. What happens on the outside is a result of having good health on the inside, including a healthy mind and spirit.

Sometimes life gives us things that we don't understand. It may never make sense, but we can still find purpose in it. If I hadn't gone through what I did and found a way to embrace the lessons in the journey, I never would have gained the perspective that today gives my life so much meaning. I would still be working forty to fifty hours per week, fighting traffic, living for the weekends, and trading most of my time for money while missing meaning in life.

Instead, I have hope, and I give hope. I own my life, and I show others how to own theirs. I live to inspire and be inspired. I am empowered, and I empower others.

We can all learn from each other and lift each other up. No matter what happens, we can always rise above and come out on top. It's a choice. I choose to live.

Melissa White

Melissa White is a psychic medium and intuitive advisor. As a child, she always felt deeply connected to the angelic and spirit realms, but was often confused as to how to express what she saw, and felt. It wasn't until a near death experience one week after giving birth to her son that she began to embrace and understand her psychic power.

In connecting with her soul's highest purpose, Melissa can share her gift of communicating with spirits. She is accurate, compassionate and works with integrity. Melissa provides healing messages for clients seeking confirmation, guidance, and peace. She is honored to be a clear channel for spirit and angels alike. Melissa's approach is warm and gentle while she delivers evidence and accurate information to assist others in not only believing their loved ones are near but also feeling and knowing it for themselves.

Find Melissa online:

www.melissawhitesacredsoul.com
info@melissawhitesacredsoul.com
https://www.facebook.com/soulsolaceintuitive/

Chapter 23

Choosing Faith Over Fear

By Melissa White

"Faith is seeing light with the heart when all the eyes can see is darkness."

I'm not sure who wrote this, but it beautifully illustrates a belief that resonates so deep within my soul. My story is about the faith that saw me through some dark times and enabled miracles to unfold right before my eyes.

I was twenty-three-years-old and had just given birth to a beautiful angelic boy. I was at home for about a week when I started having some very intense abdominal pains. They would hit me like a ton of bricks and were so painful that, at times, I couldn't walk. I visited the emergency room a few times and was dismissed as the doctors thought my pain was related to me just having given birth. I was given a dose of morphine and sent on my way.

In my heart, I knew something was very wrong. I was so exhausted as a new mom, and my emotions were all over the place, so I felt that I should trust what the doctors were telling me.

I started questioning my sanity. My family doctor was away on holidays so, after each painful episode, I would go to another care clinic, or emergency room if it were at night. It was clear to me that the doctors believed that my symptoms were psychosomatic or that I was merely seeking attention. I felt guilty; as though I was a nuisance. Keep in mind that all of this was occurring while I was experiencing extreme anxiety and struggling to learn to breastfeed my son. I also had contracted a mastitis infection in my breasts (which caused pain and fever). This occurred due to a medical error! The doctor was meant to prescribe medication to help decrease the amount of breast milk but he gave me medication that *increased* it!

In many ways, it was the perfect storm. The most embarrassing and degrading episode was when I was sent to a gynecologist for a consultation. She told me that I likely had a sexually transmitted disease. She put me on antibiotics and told me to go to the hospital if my condition worsened. I knew I didn't have an STD. I felt so frustrated by this doctor's assumptions that were based on my age. However, something inside me wouldn't allow me to speak up. It was as if my voice had disappeared. I had placed all of my trust in the people around me, and they were so clearly letting me down. It turns out that decision to remain silent up could have cost me my life.

One afternoon, my mom just happened to stop by my place. I had left the front door unlocked, which was out of character for me. I remember my son being asleep in his bassinette while I was lying on the couch. I recall feeling so lost and so desperate for help. No one was taking me seriously, and I felt myself slipping into a strange state of ambivalence. It was as though my body was giving up on me and all I wanted to do was sleep. My mom walked in and looked shocked. She told me I was as white as a ghost. In an instant, she had my son, and I packed up, and we were en-route to the hospital once again. This time, we were determined to find answers.

I don't recall much of my arrival at the hospital. It was as if I was in a fog of exhaustion and confusion. I believe they did some bloodwork and before I knew it, I was being wheeled in for emergency exploratory surgery. They still didn't know what was wrong, but it became apparent that I was extremely sick. I felt a mixture of relief and terror. I was so happy that I was being taken care of, but I was also so afraid that I wasn't going to make it. I had a strange feeling that I was on the edge of living or dying. I couldn't put it into words, but I felt it so deeply in my soul. I was so terrified of leaving my sweet baby boy! I'd waited my whole life to hold him and we'd only just met. How could I possibly leave him? My mind began jumping ahead to future milestones. Would I see his first steps, teach him to ride a bike? Would I be there to kiss his forehead and tuck him in at night? Would he get the chance to know me? I was so afraid that he might not know how much I loved him. It felt like being in a movie; totally surreal. *How could this be happening to me?* I thought. It was not the joyful bliss I had envisioned my post-partum experience would be. In fact, it was a complete nightmare. I didn't even get the chance to see my son before they ushered me off for surgical prep.

There were a few lonely minutes where I lay in the hospital bed by myself. No nurses or doctors were around. I was completely and utterly alone, and I began to cry. I felt completely helpless, anxious and afraid. Looking back, I'd have to say this was the moment of the biggest surrender of my life. I became still and silent. I prayed to God. I said the Hail Mary over and over. I closed my eyes and just breathed. I began pleading with God to allow me to stay. Within a few moments, I felt the undeniable presence of my father's parents (who had both passed away), standing right beside me on either side of the bed. It's an experience that's clearly etched in my memory. I didn't see them exactly—but I just *knew* it was them—I felt it in my bones. I had this moment of complete clarity, and I felt peace wash over me. I heard a voice say, "Just have the surgery, and you will be ok. Your son is not going to lose you, but for right now, you must be strong". I can't explain it other than to say it was profound. I went from feeling petrified to feeling secure and assured. It was like time stood still and I was given the miracle of hope. Little did I know that this experience with my grandparents would be the first of many more to come.

As if coming out of a haze, I opened my eyes. I could hear someone calling my name. I was informed that my appendix had ruptured so badly that they almost had to remove a portion of my bowel. My insides had been so infected that I wouldn't have lasted another twenty-four hours! I couldn't believe it. I was just so relieved to be alive that I didn't listen to anything else they told me. All I knew was that I was going to be ok.

The next morning, the surgeon came to see me, and I just laughed when he told me that it was a miracle that I was alive. It felt so inappropriate, but I couldn't help it. It just seemed too absurd. Several doctors had seen me and they either all dismissed me or misdiagnosed me. No one took the time to *listen*.

I spent a few days in utter shock. Even though I was in pain from the surgery, I still felt on top of the world! It was as if all of my energy and love for life had been restored. I felt profoundly grateful and forever changed.

I used to hesitate to call this a 'near death experience' because I didn't 'see the light,' and I don't recall seeing God or Jesus. It was a feeling… a knowing. This experience opened the door for me to explore my beliefs about God, my intuition, and purpose in life. As time went on, my body healed, but my soul took time. I began to feel so angry and traumatized. Although I was grateful to be alive, I also felt that I had been robbed of the first few weeks of motherhood. After a week of pain and illness, I spent another week in hospital without my son. I got to see him and visit with him, but I wasn't able to take care of him. I felt like an incompetent, neglectful mother.

When I arrived back home, I was still in pain, but I felt so happy to be reunited with my son. From that moment on, I became very aware of the sacred gift I had been given. I savored the time I got to spend just loving the ordinary days of life. I couldn't look at anything in quite the same way after what I had been through. I started being drawn to look deeper into my soul's purpose. Through being so close to death, I was given the gift of perspective. Although it was a frightening time in my life, it turned out to be so pivotal for me. My brush with death became the catalyst for huge changes in my life. The blessing in all of this was that it showed me just how strong I was. I wasn't afraid to stand up or myself any longer. I realized that I had to advocate for myself. I had to demand to be heard.

Looking back, I am so thankful that God sent my mom to my house that day. I didn't have the strength to fight for myself any longer. I will always say that my mom saved my life.

As it turns out, my grandparents showed me something very special. They showed me that I was able to communicate with the spirit world. It was something I had always felt drawn to, but I never realized that it was something I could actually *do*.

After I had recuperated, I started seeing things. Not random spirit people walking around all over the place, but energy and colors around people. I began reading more and more books on mediumship and psychic phenomena. I felt drawn to the mystical aspects of myself that had lain dormant for so long. I know that the spirit world was eager to assist me in recognizing my innate abilities. I questioned if I was just given a glimpse of that world in my time of need. Perhaps that's all it was. A near death experience. But, with time, I began to realize it was so much more than that. Over the next few years, I would be given significant signs. I found myself in the right place, at the right time, to receive the confirmation I needed. I realized my abilities were real and meant to be shared. In retrospect, it all makes sense. I had been given comfort and assurance from the spirit world when I needed it the most. The rest is history!

I've now been working as a full-time psychic medium for nearly four years, and the spirit world is as real to me as the physical. I work with both to bring love, healing, and validation to people when they need it the most. I wonder if I would have discovered this gift had it not been for the challenge presented to me all those years ago? The hardest times in my life had prepared me for this beautiful life. I am blessed, and it is faith that saw me through the uncertainty and darkness.

Conclusion

As you have reached the end of this journey with us, our wish as authors is to inspire you to dig deep and find the path to your stellar life.

I hope you felt the raw vulnerability, heart, and soul of each author and that through their words, you found bravery, strength and hope to travel your own path and include these stories in your life when you need them most. I hope this book has left you believing that there is life after traumatic experiences. You are not alone.

Most memorable among all the outstanding experiences of collaborating on this book was discovering the spirit and strength of each of my transformational co-authors. I am grateful to have worked alongside them during this journey. They are full of compassion and love. As we continue to build our legacies and model the way for others to follow, we've made friends who we'll always share a bond with.

Love is the center of the human experience, and life is meant to be a team sport.

Each author felt alone at one moment or another, due to a trauma or life-changing event. They knew they had to look within themselves for self-love, strength and the bravery to ask for help to move forward from darkness into light. We all need to move toward the light. It's the spark in your life; the fire in your stomach to know the passion that fuels you to the life you want.

If you find it hard to make time to sit and read why not purchase the audiobook version of Obstacles Equal Opportunities and listen to these inspiring words on the go!

FOLLOW
IT THRU

"Together we can discover the quiet voice in you that knows this can be the last time. This time you succeed!"

–Heather Andrews

Do you feel stuck in the chaotic spin called life? Are you maxed out, with no end in sight to the daily grind of work, kids, and activities? How did this happen? How did you get so tired that you could fall asleep at a stop light?

You are not alone! As a lifestyle strategist, I can tell you that there is a different way, a way for you to get a grip of the chaos, and harness the energy you need so you can do the activities you love, laugh and create a feeling of serenity in your life.

Are you stressed out?

Do you feel like you never have enough time?

Do you say yes when you mean NO, and then feel guilty?

How long can you stay in this cycle? If you answered yes to any of these questions, we need to talk.

I can share my knowledge of self-care and guide you through the tools of stress reduction using life strategies for time management, boundary setting, and effective communication with the result of helping you reclaim YOU in your life so you can create the stellar life you deserve.

I have been where you are and I understand. There is a different path for you.

Let's talk!

Heather Andrews

www.followitthru.com

The End

CPSIA information can be obtained
at www.ICGtesting.com
Printed in the USA
LVOW10s0217080617
537332LV00002B/2/P